Dobro došli!

Titles in this series:
Just Enough **Dutch**
Just Enough **French**
Just Enough **German**
Just Enough **Greek**
Just Enough **Hebrew**
Just Enough **Hungarian**
Just Enough **Italian**
Just Enough **Japanese**
Just Enough **Portugese**
Just Enough **Russian**
Just Enough **Scandinavian**
Just Enough **Serbo-Croat**
Just Enough **Spanish**
Just Enough **Turkish**
Multilingual Phrase Book

Just Enough
Serbo-Croat for Yugoslavia

D. L. Ellis, E. Spong

Pronunciation **Dr. J. Baldwin**

PASSPORT BOOKS
NTC/Contemporary Publishing Company

The publisher would like to thank the Yugoslav National Tourist Office for their help during the preparation of this book.

15 16 17 18 19 20 21 22 23 24 25 26   VRS/VRS   0 9 8 7 6

ISBN-13: 978-0-8442-9508-4
ISBN-10:   0-8442-9508-6

This book is printed on acid-free paper.

Contents

Using the phrase book	7
A note on the pronunciation system	8
A map of Yugoslavia	11
Everyday expressions	12
Crossing the border	14
Meeting people	16
Asking the way	20
The tourist information office	26
Accommodation	28
Hotel	28
Camping and youth hostelling	33
Rented accommodation: problem solving	38
General shopping	42
The drug store/The chemist's	42
Holiday items	46
The smoke shop	48
Buying clothes	50
Replacing equipment	54
Shop talk	56
Shopping for food	61
Bread	61
Cakes	62
Ice-cream and sweets	64
In the supermarket	66
Picnic food	69
Fruit and vegetables	72
Meat	75
Fish	77

Eating and drinking out 80
  Ordering a drink 80
  Ordering a snack 83
  In a restaurant 85

Health 92

Problems: complaints, loss, theft 97

The post office 100

Telephoning 102

Changing checks and money 104

Car travel 106

Public transport 112

Leisure 116

Asking if things are allowed 119

References 121
  Public notices 121
  Abbreviations 124
  Numbers 125
  Time 128
  Days 130
  Months and dates (including public holidays) 131
  Countries and nationalities 134
  Department store guide 137
  Conversion tables 139
  Clothing sizes 141

Do it yourself: some notes on the language 143

Index 151

Using the phrase book

- This phrase book is designed to help you get by in Croatia and Yugoslavia, to get what you want or need. It concentrates on the simplest but most effective way you can express these needs in an unfamiliar language.
- Serbo-Croat is a combination of two separate languages—Croatian and Serbian. These two languages are easily distinguished by their alphabet (Croatian uses the roman alphabet, Serbian uses the Cyrillic—see page 9), but are otherwise very similar. For convenience, we refer to "Serbo-Croat" throughout this book.
- Serbo-Croat is spoken in Croatia, Bosnia and Herzegovina and Yugoslavia. It is also widely understood in Slovenia and Macedonia, although the national languages of these independent states are Slovenian and Macedonian, respectively.
- Yugoslavia is made up of two republics (Serbia and Montenegro) and two autonomous provinces within the Republic of Serbia.
- The CONTENTS on p. 5 gives you a good idea of which section to consult for the phrase you need.
- The INDEX on p. 151 gives more detailed information about where to look for your phrase.
- When you have found the right page you will be given:
  either – the exact phrase
  or – help in making up a suitable sentence
  and – help to get the pronunciation right
- The English sentences in **bold type** will be useful for you in a variety of different situations, so they are worth learning by heart. (See also DO IT YOURSELF, p. 143.)
- Whenever possible you will find help in understanding what Yugoslav are saying to *you*, in reply to your questions.
- If you want to practise the basic nuts and bolts of the language further, look at the DO IT YOURSELF section starting on p. 143.
- Note especially these three sections:
  Everyday expressions p. 12
  Shop talk p. 56
  Public notices p. 121
  You are sure to want to refer to them most frequently.
- Once abroad, remember to make good use of the local tourist offices (see p. 26).

A note on the pronunciation system

In traveler's phrase books there is usually a pronunciation section which tries to teach English-speaking tourists how to correctly pronounce the language of the country they are visiting. This is based on the belief that in order to be understood, the speaker must have an accurate, authentic accent—that he must pronounce every last word letter-perfectly.

The authors of this book, on the other hand, wanted to devise a workable and usable pronunciation system. So they had to face the fact it is absolutely impossible for an average speaker of English who has no technical training in phonetics and phonetic transcription systems (which includes 98% of all the users of this book!) to reproduce the sounds of a foreign language with perfect accuracy, just from reading a phonetic transcription, cold—no prior background in the language. We also believe that you don't have to have perfect pronunciation in order to make yourself understood in a foreign country. After all, natives you run into will take into account that you are foreigners, and visitors, and more than likely they will feel gratified by your efforts to communicate and will probably go out of their way to try to understand you. They may even help you, and correct you, in a friendly manner. We have found, also, that visitors to a foreign country are not usually concerned with perfect pronunciation—they just want to get their message across, to communicate!

With this in mind, we have designed a pronunciation system which is of the utmost simplicity to use. This system does not attempt to give an accurate—but also problematical and tedious—representation of the sound system of the language, but instead uses common sound and letter combinations in English which are the closest to the sounds in the foreign language. In this way, the sentences transcribed for pronunciation should be read as naturally as possible, as if they were ordinary English. In no way does the user have to attempt to make the words sound "foreign." So, while to yourselves you will sound as if you are speaking ordinary English—or at least making ordinary English sounds—you will at the same time be making yourselves understood in another language. And, as the saying goes, practice makes perfect, so it is probably a good idea to repeat aloud to yourselves several times the phrases you think you are going to use, before you actually use them. This will give you greater confidence, and will also help in making yourself understood.

In Serbo-Croat, it is important to stress or emphasize the syllables in *italics*, just as you would if we were to take as an English example: *Little* Jack *Horner* sat in the corner. Here we have ten syllables but only four stresses.

Of course you may enjoy trying to pronounce a foreign language as well as possible and the present system is a good way to start. However, since it uses only the sounds of English, you will very soon need to depart from it as you imitate the sounds you hear the native speaker produce and relate them to the spelling of the other language.

For interest, below you will find the characters of the Cyrillic alphabet which you will probably not need but which is used throughout Yugoslavia – but not in Croatia where the Roman alphabet is in use. The columns on the left show the printed capital and small letters, and the one on the right the corresponding letter in the Roman alphabet (as used in this book).

А	а	a	Г	г	g	О	о	o
Б	б	b	Х	х	h	П	п	p
Ц	ц	c	И	и	i	Р	р	r
Ч	ч	č	Ј	ј	j	С	с	s
Ћ	ħ	ć	К	к	k	Ш	ш	š
Д	д	d	Л	л	l	Т	т	t
Џ	и	dž	Љ	љ	lj	У	у	u
Ђ	ђ	dj	М	м	m	В	в	v
Е	е	e	Н	н	n	З	з	z
Ф	ф	f	Њ	њ	nj	Ж	ж	ž

Dobra zabava!

Countries and main towns

Everyday expressions

[See also 'Shop talk', p. 56]

Hello (informal)	**Zdravo** zdra-fo
Good morning	**Dobro jutro** dob-ro yootro
Good day (hello)	**Dobar dan** dob-ar dun
Good night	**Laku noć** la-koo noch
Goodbye	**Zbogom** zbog-om
See you later	**Dovidjenja** doveejen-ya
Yes	**Da** da
Please	**Molim** mol-im
Yes, please	**Da, molim** da mol-im
Great!	**Divno!** deev-no
Thank you	**Hvala vam** fa-la vum
Thank you very much	**Puno vam hvala** poono vum fa-la
That's right	**Točno** toch-no
No	**Ne** neh
No, thank you	**Ne, hvala** neh fa-la
I disagree	**Ne slažem se** neh sla-shem seh
Excuse me ⎤ Sorry	**Oprostite/pardon** oprost-eet-eh/par-don
Don't mention it ⎤ That's OK	**Molim** mol-im
That's good ⎤ I like it	**Dobro je** dob-ro jeh

That's no good ⎤	**Nije dobro**
I don't like it ⎦	nee-yeh dob-ro
I know	**Znam**
	znum
I don't know	**Ne znam**
	neh znum
It doesn't matter	**Ne smeta**
	neh smeh-ta
Where's the toilet, please?	**Gdje je toaleta, molim?**
	gd-yeh yeh twa-leh-ta mol-im
How much is that? [point]	**Koliko to košta?**
	kol-eeko toh koshta
Is the service included?	**Da li je servis uračunat?**
	da lee yeh sairvis oora-choo-nat
Do you speak English?	**Govorite li engleski?**
	gov-oree-teh lee en-glesky
I'm sorry . . .	**Žao mi je . . .**
	sha-o mee yeh . . .
I don't speak Serbo-Croat	**ne govorim srpsko-hrvatski**
	neh gov-oreem serpsko-hrvatsky
I only speak a little Serbo-Croat	**govorim samo malo srpsko-hrvatski**
	gov-oreem sa-mo mai-lo serpsko-hrvatsky
I don't understand	**ne razumjem**
	neh razoom-yem
Please can you . . .	**Molim vas, možete li . . .**
	mol-im vus mosh-et-eh lee . . .
repeat that?	**to ponoviti?**
	toh pono-veetee
speak more slowly?	**govoriti polaganije?**
	gov-oreetee pola-gan-ee-yeh
write it down?	**napisati?**
	napeesat-ee
What is this called in Serbo-Croat? [point].	**Kako se zove ovo u srpsko-hrvatskom jeziku?**
	ka-ko seh zhov-eh ov-o oo serp sko hervat-skom yez-eekoo

Crossing the border

ESSENTIAL INFORMATION

- Don't waste time just before you leave rehearsing what you're going to say to the border officials – the chances are that you won't have to say anything at all, especially if you travel by air.
- It's more useful to check that you have your documents handy for the journey: passport, tickets, money, travellers' cheques, insurance documents, driving licence and car registration documents.
- Look out for these signs:
  CARINARNICA (customs)
  GRANICA (border)
  GRANIČNA MILICIJA (frontier police)
  [*For further signs and notices, see p. 121*]
- You may be asked routine questions by the customs officials [*see below*]. If you have to give personal details see 'Meeting people', p. 16. The other important answer to know is 'Nothing': **Ništa** (*neesh*-ta).

ROUTINE QUESTIONS

Passport?	**Pasoš?**
	p*as*-osh
Insurance?	**Osiguranje?**
	oseegoo-*ran*-yeh
Registration document? (logbook)	**Saobraćajnu knjižicu**
	sa-*o*bracha-eenoo kn-y*ee*-shee-tsoo
Ticket, please	**Kartu, molim**
	k*ar*too m*o*l-im
Have you anything to declare?	**Imate li išta za prijaviti?**
	*ee*mat-eh lee *ee*sh-ta za pr*ee*-ya-veet-ee
Where are you going?	**Gdje idete?**
	gd-y*eh* *ee*det-eh
How long are you staying?	**Koliko ćete se zadrzati?**
	k*o*l-eeko chet-eh seh zad*er*-shatee
Where have you come from?	**Odakle dolazite?**
	*o*d*a*k-leh d*o*laz-eet*eh*

You may also have to fill in forms which ask for:

surname	**prezime**
first name	**ime**
place of birth	**mjesto rodjenja**
date of birth	**datum rodjenja**
address	**adresa**
nationality	**narodnost**
profession	**zanimanje**
passport number	**broj pasoša**
issued at	**izdan u**
signature	**potpis**

Meeting people

[*See also 'Everyday expressions', p. 12*]

Breaking the ice

Hello	**Dobar dan**
	dob-ar dun
Good morning	**Dobro jutro**
	dob-ro yootro
How are you?	**Kako ste?**
	ka-ko steh
Pleased to meet you	**Drago mi je upoznati vas**
	dra-go mee yeh oopozna-tee vus
I am here . . .	**Ovdje sam . . .**
	ovd-yeh sum . . .
on holiday	**na odmoru**
	na odmoroo
on business	**poslovno**
	poslov-no
Can I offer you . . .	**Mogu li vam ponuditi . . .**
	mog-oo lee vum pon-oodeetee . . .
a drink?	**nešto za piti?**
	nesh-to za peetee
a cigarette?	**cigaretu?**
	tseega-reh-too
a cigar?	**cigar?**
	tseegar
Are you staying long?	**Hoćete li se zadržati dugo?**
	hoch-et-eh lee seh zader-shatee doogo

Name

What's your name?	**Kako se zovete?**
	ka-ko seh zov-et-eh
My name is . . .	**Ja se zovem . . .**
	ya seh zov-em . . .

Family

Are you married?	**Da li ste oženjen/udata*?**
	da lee steh oshen-yen/ooda-ta?
I am . . .	**Ja sam . . .**
	ya sum . . .
married	**oženjen/udata***
	oshen-yen/ooda-ta
single	**neoženjen/neudata***
	neh-oshen-yen/neh-ood-ata
This is . . .	**Ovo je . . .**
	ov-o yeh . . .
my wife	**moja žena**
	moya shen-a
my husband	**moj muž**
	moy moosh
my son	**moj sin**
	moy seen
my daughter	**moja kćerka**
	moya chairka
my (boy) friend	**moj mladić**
	moy mlad-eech
my (girl) friend	**moja djevojka**
	moya dee-yev-oy-ka
my (male) colleague	**moj kolega**
	moy kol-ega
my (female) colleague	**moja kolegica**
	moya kol-eg-eetsa
Do you have any children?	**Imate li djece?**
	eemat-eh lee dee-yets-eh
I have . . .	**Imam . . .**
	eem-am . . .
one daughter	**jednu kćerku**
	yed-noo chair-koo
one son	**jednog sina**
	yed-nog seena
two daughters	**dvije kćerke**
	dvee-yeh chair-keh
three sons	**tri sina**
	tree seena

*For men use the first alternative, for women the second

No, I haven't any children	**Nemam djece**
	nem-am dee-yets-eh

Where you live

Are you . . .	**Jeste li . . .**
	yest-eh lee . . .
Italian?	**Talijan/Talijanka*?**
	tal*ee*-yan/tal*ee*-yanka
Swiss?	**Švajcarac/Švajcarka*?**
	shvay-t*sa*-rats/shvay-t*sa*rka
Yugoslav?	**Yugoslaven/Yugoslavenka*?**
	yoogo-sl*a*-ven/
	yoogo-sl*a*-venka
I am . . .	**Ja sam . . .**
	ya sum . . .
American	**Amerikanac/Amerikanka***
	amerik*a*-nats/amerik*a*nka
English	**Englez/Engleskinja***
	en-glez/en-glez-keen-ya

[*For other nationalities, see p. 136*]

I am . . .	**Ja sam . . .**
	ya sum . . .
from London	**iz Londona**
	eez l*o*nd-ona
from England	**iz Engleske**
	eez *e*n-gles-keh
from the north	**sa sjevera**
	sa see-*ev*-era
from the south	**sa juga**
	sa y*oo*ga
from the east	**sa istoka**
	sa *ee*st-oka
from the west	**sa zapada**
	sa z*a*pada
from the centre	**iz centra**

[*For other countries, see p. 134*] eez tsen-tra

*For men use the first alternative, for women the second

For the businessman and woman

I work for . . . (firm's name)	**Ja radim za . . .**
	ya rad-eem za . . .
I have an appointment with . . .	**Imam sastanak sa . . .**
	eem-am sast-anak sa . . .
May I speak to . . . ?	**Mogu li govoriti sa . . . ?**
	mog-oo lee gov-oree-tee sa . . .
This is my card	**Ovo je moja posjetnica**
	ov-o yeh moya pos-yet-nitsa
I'm sorry, I'm late	**Oprostite, zakasnio sam**
	oprost-eet-eh zakas-nee-o sum
Can I fix another appointment?	**Mogu li ugovoriti drugi sastanak?**
	mog-oo lee oogovo-reetee droog-ee sast-anak
I'm staying . . .	**Ja sam odseo/odsjela* . . .**
	ya sum ods-yeh-o/ods-yel-a . . .
at the hotel (Belgrade)	**u hotel Beograd?**
	oo hotel beh-ograd
in (Rebublic) square	**na trgu (Republike)**
	na tergoo (repub-leeke)

*For men use the first alternative, for women the second

Asking the way

ESSENTIAL INFORMATION

● Keep a look out for all these place names as you will find them on shops, maps and notices.

WHAT TO SAY

Excuse me, please

Oprostite, molim
oprost-eet-eh mol-im

Which is the way . . .

Koji je put . . .
koyee yeh poot . . .

to Belgrade?

za Beograd?
za beh-ograd

to (Republic) street?

za ulicu (Republike)?
za ooleetsoo (repoob-leekeh)

to the Hotel Lapad?

za Hotel Lapad?
za hotel lap-ad

to the airport?

za aerodrom?
za ah-airodrom

to the beach?

za plažu?
za plash-oo

to the bus station?

za autobusnu stanicu?
za ah-ooto-boosnoo stan-eetsoo

to the historic site?

za historijsko mjesto?
za heestoree-sko m-yesto

to the market?

za tržnicu?
za ter-shnee-tsoo

to the police station?

za miliciju?
za meel-eets-yoo

to the port?

za luku?
za loo-koo

to the post office?

za poštu?
za posh-too

to the railway station?

za željezničku stanicu?
za shel-yezneech-koo stan-eetsoo

to the sports stadium?

za športski stadion?
za shport-skee stad-ee-on

to the tourist information office	**za turistički ured?**
	za *t*oorist-eech-kee *oo*-red
to the town centre?	**za centar grada?**
	za tsen-tar gr*a*-da
to the town hall?	**za gradsku općinu?**
	za gr*a*t-skoo *o*p-chee-noo
Excuse me, please	**Oprostite, molim**
	oprost-eet-eh m*o*l-im
Is there . . . near by?	**Ima li ovdje blizu . . .?**
	*ee*ma lee *o*vd-yeh bl*ee*-zoo . . .
an art gallery?	**umjetnička galerija?**
	*oo*myet-neech-ka gal*ai*r-eeya
a baker's	**pekarna**
	p*e*k-arna
a bank	**banka**
	b*a*n-ka
a botanical garden	**botanički vrt**
	b*o*t-aneech-kee v*e*rt
a bus stop	**autobusna stanica**
	*a*h-ooto-boosna st*a*n-eetsa
a butcher's	**mesarnica**
	mes*a*r-neetsa
a café	**kavana**
	kav*a*-na
a cake shop	**slastičarna**
	slastee-ch*a*rna
a campsite	**autokamp**
	*a*h-ooto-kamp
a car park	**parkiralište**
	par-k*ee*-ral-eeshteh
a change bureau	**mjenjačnica**
	m-hyen-y*a*ch-neetsa
a chemist's	**apoteka**
	apot*e*k-ah
a church	**crkva**
	ts*e*rk-va
a cinema	**kino**
	k*ee*no
a concert hall	**dvorana za koncerte**
	dvor*a*-na za k*o*n-tsairteh
a delicatessen	**delikatesna radnja**
	delikat*e*s-na r*a*dn-ya

Is there . . . near by?	**Ima li ovdje blizu . . .?**
	eema lee ovd-yeh bleezoo . . .
a dentist's	**zubar**
	zoobar
a department store	**robna kuća**
	robna koocha
a disco	**disko klub**
	disko-cloob
a doctor's surgery	**liječnička ordinacija**
	lee-yech-neechka ordeen-atsee-ya
a dry cleaner's	**kemijska čistiona**
	kem-eeska cheest-yona
a fishmonger's	**ribarnica**
	reebar-neetsa
a garage (for repairs)	**garaža**
	gara-sha
a hairdresser's	**frizer**
	freez-air
a greengrocer's	**voćarna**
	voch-arna
a grocer's	**dućan mješovite robe**
	doochan m-yesh-oveeteh robeh
a hardware shop	**željezara**
	shel-yez-ara
a hospital	**bolnica**
	bol-nitsa
a hotel	**hotel**
	hotel
an ice-cream parlour	**slastičarna**
	slasti-charna
a laundry	**praonica**
	pra-on-eetsa
a museum	**muzej**
	moo-zay
a newsagent's	**prodavaona novina**
	prodava-ona novee-na
a night club	**noćni lokal**
	nochni lok-al
a park	**park**
	park
a petrol station	**benzinska stanica**
	benzeen-ska stan-eetsa

a post box	**poštanski sandučić**
	poshtan-skee sand-*oo*chitch
a public garden	**park**
	park
a restaurant	**restoran**
	rest-oran
a snack bar	**snek bar**
	snack bar
a sports ground	**športsko igralište**
	shport-sko eegra-*lee*shteh
a supermarket	**supermarket/robna kuća**
	supermarket/robna k*oo*cha
a swimming pool	**bazen**
	b*a*z-en
a taxi stand	**stajalište taksija**
	st*a*-yal*ee*sh-teh t*a*k-see-ya
a telephone	**telefon**
	t*e*lephon
a theatre	**kazalište**
	k*a*z-al*ee*shteh
a tobacconist's	**trafika**
	tr*a*f-eeka
a toilet	**toaleta**
	tw*a*-leh-ta
a travel agent's	**putna agencija**
	p*oo*tna agents*ee*-ya
a youth hostel	**omladinski dom**
	*o*mlad-een-skee dom
a zoo	**zoološki vrt**
	z*oo*-losh-kee vert.

[*continued over*]

DIRECTIONS

- Asking where a place is, or if a place is near by, is one thing; making sense of the answer is another.
- Here are some of the most important key directions and replies.

Left	**Lijevo** lee-yev-o
Right	**Desno** desno
Straight on	**Ravno** ravno
There	**Tamo** tamo
First left/right	**Prva na lijevo/na desno** perva na lee-yev-o/na desno
Second left/right	**Druga na lijevo/na desno** drooga na lee-yev-o/na desno
At the crossroads	**Na raskrsnici** na rasker-snee-tsee
At the traffic lights	**Na prometna svijetla** na prom-etna svee-yet-la
At the roundabout	**Na kružnicu** na kroosh-nee-tsoo
At the level crossing	**Na prijelaz preko pruge** na pree-yel-az prek-o proog-eh
It's near/far	**Blizu je/daleko je** bleez-oo yeh/da-lek-o yeh
One kilometre	**Jedan kilometar** yed-an keelo-met-ar
Two kilometres	**Dva kilometra** dva keelo-metra
Five minutes . . .	**Pet minuta . . .** pet meen-oota . . .
on foot	**pješke** p-yesh-keh
by car	**sa kolima** sa kol-eema

Take . . .

    the bus

    the train

    the tram

Uzmite . . .
ooz-mee-teh . . .
autobus
ah-ooto-boos
vlak
vlak
tramvaj
tramva-ee

[*For public transport, see p. 112*]

The tourist information office

ESSENTIAL INFORMATION

- Most towns and even some coastal villages in Croatia and Yugoslavia have a tourist information office.
- Look for these words:
  TURISTIČKI INFORMATIVNI CENTAR
  TURISTIČKI URED
  TURISTIČKA AGENCIJA ZA INFORMACIJE
- Sometimes there may be signposts with these abbreviations: **TIC**
- These offices offer you free information in the form of printed leaflets, fold-outs, brochures, lists and plans.
- You may have to pay for some documents but this is not usual.
- For finding a tourist office, see p. 20.

WHAT TO SAY

Please, have you got . . .	**Molim, imate li . . .** mol-im *eema*-teh lee . . .
a plan of the town?	**plan grada?** plan gra-da
a list of hotels?	**katalog hotela?** katalog hotel-a
a list of campsites?	**katalog autokampova?** katalog *ah*-ooto-kampova
a list of restaurants?	**katalog restorana?** katalog restora-na
a list of coach excursions?	**katalog izleta sa autobusom?** katalog *eez*-let-a sa *ah*-ootoboos-om
a list of events?	**katalog zabava?** katalog zab-ava
a leaflet on the town?	**prospekt grada?** prospekt gra-da
a leaflet on the region?	**prospekt pokrajine?** prospect pokra-yeeneh
a railway timetable?	**red vožnje?** red vosh-nee-yeh
a bus timetable?	**red autobusa?** red *ah*-ooto-boosa

In English, please	**Na engleskom jeziku, molim**
	na en-gles-kom yez-eekoo
	mol-im
How much do I owe you?	**Koliko to košta**
	ko-leeko toh koshta
Can you recommend . . .	**Možete li preporučiti . . .**
	mosh-et-eh lee preporoo-chit-ee . . .
a cheap hotel?	**jeftin hotel?**
	yef-teen hotel
a cheap restaurant?	**jeftin restoran?**
	yef-teen rest-oran?
Can you make a booking for me?	**Možete li rezervirati za mene?**
	mosh-et-eh lee rezair-veer-atee za meh-neh?

LIKELY ANSWERS

You need to understand when the answer is 'No'. You should be able to tell by the assistant's facial expression, tone of voice and gesture; but there are some language clues, such as:

No	**Ne**
	neh
I'm sorry	**Žao mi je**
	sha-o mee yeh
I don't have a list of campsites	**Nemam katalog autokampova**
	neh-mum katalog ah-ooto-kampova
I haven't got any left	**Nemam ni jednog više**
	neh-mum nee yed-nog veesheh
It's free	**To je besplatno**
	toh yeh bes-plat-no

Accommodation

Hotel

ESSENTIAL INFORMATION

- If you want hotel-type accommodation, all the following words in capital letters are worth looking for on name boards:
  HOTEL
  MOTEL
  PANSION (superior boarding house)
- Houses which let rooms privately usually have signs in French, English, German or Italian:
  CHAMBRES/ROOMS/ZIMMER/CAMERE
  Remember that:
- A list of hotels in the town or district can usually be obtained at the local tourist information office [see p. 26].
- Hotels are divided into five classes, pensions into three.
- Not all hotels provide meals, apart from breakfast. (A pension always provides meals). However, for stays of more than three days, hotels and pensions have fixed prices which include accommodation, three meals a day and whatever services are available.
- The cost is displayed in the room itself so you can check it when having a look around before agreeing to stay.
- The displayed cost is for the room itself, per night and not per person.
- Breakfast usually consists of coffee, milk, tea or cocoa with rolls or toast, butter and jam or honey.
- On arrival you will be asked to complete a registration document and the receptionist will want to see your passport and travel documents.
- Tipping is not obligatory but 10% is usual.
- Finding a hotel, see p. 20.

WHAT TO SAY

I have a booking	**Imam rezervirano**
	eem-am rezair-veer-ano
Have you any vacancies, please?	**Imate li praznu sobu, molim?**
	eemat-eh lee praz-noo so-boo mol-im
Can I book a room?	**Mogu li rezervirati sobu?**
	mog-oo lee rezair-veer-atee so-boo
It's for . . .	**To je za . . .**
	toh yeh za . . .
one person	**jednu osobu**
	yed-noo os-oboo
two people	**dvije osobe**
[For numbers, see p. 125]	*dvee-yeh os-obeh*
It's for . . .	**To je za . . .**
	toh yeh za . . .
one night	**jednu noć**
	yed-noo noch
two nights	**dvije noći**
	dvee-yeh nochee
one week	**jednu sedmicu**
	yed-noo sedmee-tsoo
two weeks	**dvije sedmice**
	dvee-yeh sedmee-tseh
I would like . . .	**Želio/željela* bih . . .**
	shel-yo/shel-yel-ah beeh . . .
one room	**jednu sobu**
	yed-noo so-boo
two rooms	**dvije sobe**
	dvee-yeh so-beh
with a single bed	**jednokrevetnu**
	yed-nokrev-et-noo
with two single beds	**dvokrevetnu sa odvojenim krevetima**
	dvo-krev-et-noo sa odvo-yen-eem krev-et-eema
with a double bed	**dvokrevetnu**
	dvo-krev-et-noo
with a toilet	**sa toaletom**
	sa twa-leh-tom

*Men use the first alternative, women the second

I would like . . .(a room)	**Želio/željela* bih. . .(sobu)**
	shel-yo/shel-yel-ah beeh. . .(so-boo)
with a bathroom	**sa kupatilom**
	sa koo-pat-eelom
with a shower	**sa tušom**
	sa too-shom
with a cot	**sa dječjim krevetom**
	sa dee-yech-eem krev-et-om
with a balcony	**sa balkonom**
	sa balkon-om
I would like . . .	**Želio/željela* bih . . .**
	shel-yo/shel-yel-ah beeh . . .
full board	**sa punim pansionom**
	sa poon-eem pansee-onòm
bed and breakfast	**sobu i doručak**
	so-boo ee doroo-chak
Do you serve meals?	**Servirate li jela?**
	sairv-eerat-eh lee yel-ah
At what time is . . .	**U koliko sati je . . .**
	oo kol-eeko sa-tee yeh . . .
breakfast?	**doručak**
	doroo-chak
lunch?	**ručak?**
	roochak
dinner?	**večera?**
	vech-era
How much is it?	**Koliko je to?**
	kol-eeko yeh toh
Can I look at the room?	**Mogu li da vidim sobu?**
	mog-oo lee da vee-deem so-boo
I'd prefer a room . . .	**Više volim sobu . . .**
	vee-sheh vol-im so-boo . . .
at the front/at the back	**sa pogledom na ulicu/dvorište**
	sa pog-led-om na ool-itsoo dvoreesh-teh
OK, I'll take it	**Dobro je, uzeti ću je**
	dobro yeh ooz-et-ee choo yeh
No thanks, I won't take it	**Ne hvala, neću je uzeti**
	neh fa-la neh-choo yeh ooz-etee
The key to number (10), please	**Ključ za sobu broj (deset), molim**
	klee-yooch za so-boo broy (deh-set) mol-im

*Men use the first alternative, women the second

Please, may I have ...	**Molim, mogu li dobiti ...**
	mol-im mogoo lee dob-eetee ...
a coat hanger?	**vješalicu?**
	vee-yesha-leetsoo
a towel?	**ručnik?**
	rooch-nik
a glass?	**čašu?**
	chash-oo
some soap?	**sapun?**
	sap-oon
an ashtray?	**pepeljaru?**
	pep-el-yar-oo
another pillow?	**još jedan jastuk?**
	yosh yed-an yas-took
another blanket?	**još jedan pokrivač?**
	yosh yed-an pok-reevach
Come in!	**Uđite!**
	oo-jee-teh
One moment, please!	**Načas, molim!**
	na-chas mol-im
Please can you ...	**Molim, možete li ...**
	mol-im mosh-et-eh lee ...
do this laundry/dry cleaning?	**oprati/očistiti kemijski?**
	opra-tee/ocheest-ee-tee kem-ee-skee
call me at ...?	**me zvati u ...?**
	meh zvah-tee oo ...
help me with my luggage?	**mi pomoći sa mojom prtljagon?**
	mee pom-ochee sa moyom pertl-ya-gom
call me a taxi for ...?	**mi zvati taksi za ...?**
	mee zva-tee taxi za ...

[*For times, see p. 128*]

The bill, please	**Račun, molim**
	rach-oon mol-im
Is service included?	**Je li servis uračunat?**
	yeh lee sairvis oorach-oonat
I think this is wrong	**Mislim da ovo nije točno**
	meeslim da o-vo nee-yeh toch-no
May I have a receipt?	**Želio/željela* bih priznanicu**
	shel-yo/shel-yeh-ah beeh preeznan-eetsoo

*Men use the first alternative, women the second

At breakfast

Some more . . . please	**Malo više . . . molim**
	ma-lo veesh-eh . . . mol-im
coffee	**kave**
	ka-veh
tea	**čaja**
	cha-ya
bread	**kruha**
	kroo-ha
butter	**maslaca**
	mas-la-tsa
marmalade	**marmelade**
	marmela-deh
jam	**djem**
	jam
May I have a soft boiled egg?	**Želio/željela* bih meko kuhano jaje?**
	shel-yo/shel-yel-ah beeh mek-o koo-ha-no ya-yeh

LIKELY REACTIONS

Have you an identity document, please?	**Imate li ličnu legitimaciju, molim?**
	eemat-eh lee leech-noo leg-eetee-matsee mol-im
What's your name [see p. 16]	**Kako se zovete?**
	ka-ko seh zov-et-eh
Sorry, we're full	**Žao mi je ali smo puni**
	sha-o mee yeh ah-lee smo poon-ee
I haven't any rooms left	**Nemam niti jednu sobu praznu**
	neh-mum neetee yed-noo so-boo praz-noo
Do you want to have a look?	**Hoćete li da vidite?**
	hoch-et-eh lee da veed-eet-eh
How many people is it for?	**Za koliko osoba?**
	za kol-eeko os-oba
From (seven o'clock) onwards	**Od (sedam sati) unaprijed**
	od (seh-dam sat-ee) oona-pree-yed
From (midday) onwards	**Od (podne) unaprijed**
[For times, see p. 128]	od (podneh) oona-pree-yed
It's . . . dinars	**To je . . . dinara**
[For numbers, see p. 125]	toh yeh . . . deena-ra

*Men use the first alternative, women the second

Camping and youth hostelling

ESSENTIAL INFORMATION
Camping

- Look for the words: **KAMPING** or **AUTO-CAMP** or this sign.

- Be prepared for the following charges
  per person
  for the car (if applicable)
  for the tent or caravan plot
  for electricity
  for hot showers
- You must provide proof of identity, such as your passport.
- All campsites are state owned and state controlled.
- If you wish to camp off-site, you must obtain a permit from the local tourist office or the municipality.
- On some sites, accommodation is also available in chalets.

Youth hostels

- Look for the word: **OMLADINSKI DOM**
- You must have a YHA card.
- Accommodation is usually provided in small dormitories and you should take your own sleeping bag lining with you.
- Food and cooking facilities vary from place to place and you may also have to help with the domestic chores.
- Accommodation is also available in the student hotels to be found in larger towns which are run by **FERIJALNI SAVEZ** (Yugoslav Youth School Organization) and **HRVATSKI FERIJALNI I HOSTELSKI SAVEZ** (Croatian Youth Hostel Association).
- **NAROMTRAVEL** which specializes in travel and holidays for young people and students in Yugoslavia also runs its own international youth centres.
- Finding a campsite and a youth hostel, see p. 20
- Replacing equipment, see p. 54.

WHAT TO SAY

I have a booking	**Imam rezervirano** *eem*-am rezair-*veer*-ano
Have you any vacancies?	**Imate li mjesta?** *ee*mat-eh lee m-*yes*ta
It's for . . .	**To je za . . .** toh yeh za . . .
one adult	**jednu osoby** yed-noo *o*s-oboo
two adults	**dvije osobu** dv*ee*-yeh *o*s-obeh
and one child	**i jedno dijete** ee yedno dee-*yet*-eh
and two children	**i dvoje djece** ee dv*o*-yeh dee-*yets*eh
It's for . . .	**To je za . . .** toh yeh za . . .
one night	**jednu noć** yed-noo n*o*ch
two nights	**dvije noći** dv*ee*-yeh n*o*chee
one week	**jednu sedmicu** yed-noo s*e*d-mee-tsoo
two weeks	**dvije sedmice** dv*ee*-yeh s*e*d-mee-tseh
How much is it . . .	**Koliko je . . .** k*o*l-eeko yeh . . .
for the tent?	**za šator?** za sh*a*-tor
for the caravan (trailer)?	**za karavanu?** za karav*a*noo
for the car?	**za kola?** za k*o*la
for the electricity?	**za struju?** za str*oo*-yoo
per person?	**po osobi?** po *o*s-obee
per day/night?	**na dan/noć?** na d*u*n/n*o*ch
May I look round?	**Mogu li pogledati okolo?** m*o*g-oo lee p*o*gleh-da-tee *o*kolo
Do you close at night?	**Kada zatvarate noću?** k*a*-da z*a*tvarat-eh n*o*choo

Do you provide anything . . .	**Mogu li nabaviti nešto . . .**
	m*o*g-oo lee n*a*-bav-eetee n*e*sh-to . . .
to eat?	**za jesti?**
	za *ye*s-tee
to drink?	**za piti?**
	za p*ee*tee
Do you have . . .	**Imate li . . .**
	*ee*mat-eh lee . . .
a bar?	**bar?**
	bar
hot showers?	**vrući tuš?**
	vr*oo*-chee toosh
a kitchen?	**kuhinju?**
	k*oo*-heen-yoo
a laundry?	**praonicu?**
	pra-*o*nee-tsoo
a restaurant?	**restoran?**
	r*e*st-oran
a shop?	**dućan?**
	d*oo*ch-an
a swimming pool?	**bazen?**
	b*a*z-en
a takeaway?	**snak-bar?**
	snack bar

[*For food shopping, see p. 61, and for eating and drinking out, see p. 80*]

Where are . . .	**Gdje su . . .**
	gd-*ye*h soo . . .
the dustbins?	**kante za smeće?**
	k*a*nteh za sm*e*h-cheh
the showers?	**tuševi?**
	t*oo*shev-ee
the toilets?	**toalete?**
	twa-leh-teh
At what time must one . . .	**U koliko sati se mora . . .**
	oo k*o*l-eeko s*a*-tee seh m*o*ra . . .
go to bed?	**ići spavati?**
	*ee*chee sp*a*va-tee
get up?	**ustati?**
	*oo*sta-tee

Is there . . .	**Ima li tu . . .**
	*ee*ma lee too . . .
a broom?	**metla?**
	m*e*tla
a corkscrew?	**vadičep?**
	v*a*-deechep
a drying-up cloth?	**kanavac za sušenje?**
	kan*a*-vats za s*oo*sh-en-yeh
a fork?	**vilica?**
	v*ee*l-eetsa
a fridge?	**frižider?**
	frig*i*d-air
a frying pan?	**tavica?**
	t*a*v-eetsa
an iron?	**pegla?**
	p*e*gla
a knife?	**nož?**
	nosh
a plate?	**tanjur?**
	t*a*n-yoor
a saucepan?	**lonac?**
	l*o*n-ats
a teaspoon?	**mala žlica?**
	m*a*-la shl*ee*-tsa
a tin opener?	**otvarač za konzervu?**
	otvar-ach za konz*ai*r-voo
any washing powder?	**prašak za pranje?**
	pr*a*sh-ak za pr*a*n-yeh
any washing-up liquid?	**tekućina za pranje?**
	tekooch-*ee*na za pr*a*n-yeh
The bill, please	**Račun, molim**
	r*a*ch-oon m*o*l-im

Problems

The toilet	**Toaleta**
	tw*a*-leh-ta
The shower	**Tuš**
	t*oo*sh
The tap	**Slavina**
	sl*a*v-eena
The electric point	**Utikač**
	*oo*teek-ach

The light	**Svijetlo**
	svee-yetlo
. . . is not working	**. . . ne radi**
	neh ra-dee
My camping gas has run out	**Nestalo mi je plina**
	neh-stalo mee yeh plee-na

LIKELY REACTIONS

Have you an identity document?	**Imate li legitimaciju?**
	eemat-eh lee leg-eetee-matsee-yoo
Your membership card, please	**Vašu člansku kartu, molim**
	vashoo chlan-skoo kartoo mol-im
What's your name, please? [see p. 16]	**Vaše ime molim?**
	vasheh eemeh mol-im
Sorry, we're full	**Žao mi je ali smo puni**
	sha-o mee yeh ah-lee smo poonee
How many people is it for?	**Za koliko osoba?**
	za kol-eeko os-oba
How many nights is it for?	**Za koliko noći?**
	za kol-eeko nochee
It's . . . dinars	**To je . . . dinara**
	toh yeh . . . deena-ra
per day/per night [For numbers, see p. 125]	**na dan/na noć**
	na dun/na noch

Rented accommodation: problem solving

ESSENTIAL INFORMATION

- If you're looking for accommodation to rent, watch for the following signs:
  IZNAJMIVA SE (for rent)
  IZNAJMLJUJE SE (for rent)
  APARTMANI (apartments)
  SOBE (rooms)
  VILE (villas)
- For arranging details of your let, see 'Hotel', p. 28
- Key words you will meet if renting on the spot:
  depozit (deposit)
  depozit
  ključ (key)
  klee-*yooch*
- Having arranged your own accommodation and arrived with the key, check the obvious basics that you take for granted at home.
  Electricity Voltage? Razors and small appliances brought from home may need adjusting. You may need an adaptor. All light bulbs in Yugoslavia are of the screw-in type, and all plugs have round pins.
  Gas Town gas or bottled gas? Butane gas must be kept indoors, propane gas must be kept outdoors.
  Cooker Don't be surprised to find:
  – the grill inside the oven, or no grill at all.
  – a lid covering the rings which lifts up to form a 'splash-back'
  – a mixture of two gas rings and two electric rings.
  Toilet Mains drainage or septic tank? *Don't* flush disposable nappies or anything else down the toilet, as drainage pipes are very narrow and easily blocked.
  Water Find the stopcock. Check taps and plugs – they may not operate in the way you are used to. Check how to turn on (or light) the hot water.
  Windows Check the method of opening and closing windows and shutters.
  Insects Is an insecticide spray provided? If not, get one locally.
  Equipment For buying or replacing equipment, see p. 54.
- You will probably have an official agent, but be clear in your own mind who to contact in an emergency, even if it is only a neighbour in the first instance.

WHAT TO SAY

My name is . . .	**Moje ime je . . .** moyeh *ee*meh yeh . . .
I'm staying at . . .	**Odsjeo/odsjela* sam u . . .** od-yeh-o/ods-yel-ah sum oo
They've cut off . . .	**Prekinuli su . . .** prek-*ee*noo-lee soo . . .
the electricity	**struju** str*oo*-yoo
the gas	**plin** pl*ee*n
the water	**vodu** vod-oo
Is there . . . in the area?	**Imali ovdje blizu . . .** *ee*ma lee ovd-yeh bl*ee*-zoo . . .
an electrician	**električar?** *e*l-*e*ktree-char?
a plumber	**vodoinstalater?** vod-o-insta-la-ter
a gas fitter	**plinar?** pl*ee*nar
Where is . . .	**Gdje je . . .** gd-yeh yeh . . .
the fuse box?	**električni osigurač?** *e*l-*e*ktreechnee oseeg*oo*-rach?
the stopcock?	**ventil?** ven-teel?
the boiler?	**bojler?** b*oi*ler?
the water heater?	**grijač za vodu?** gr*ee*-yach za vod-oo?
Is there . . .	**Ima li . . .** *ee*ma lee . . .
town gas?/bottled gas?	**gradski plin?/plin u bocama?** grat-skee pl*ee*n/pl*ee*n oo botsama?
mains drainage?	**kanalizacija?** kanalee*za*-tsee-ya
a septic tank?	**septična jama?** sept eech-na ya-ma
central heating?	**centralno grijanje?** tsentral-no gr*ee*-yan-yeh

*Men use the first alternative, women the second

The cooker	**Peć za kuhanje**
	pech za koo-han-yeh
The hairdryer	**Fen za kosu**
	fen za kos-oo
The heating	**Grijanje**
	gree-yan-yeh
The iron	**Pegla**
	pegla
The pilot light	**Kontrolno svijetlo**
	kontrol-no svee-yetlo
The refrigerator	**Frižider**
	frigid-air
The telephone	**Telefon**
	telephon
The toilet	**Toaleta**
	twa-leh-ta
The washing machine	**Stroj za pranje rublja**
	stroy za pran-yeh roobl-ya
The water heater	**Bojler**
	boiler
. . . is not working	**. . . ne radi**
	. . . neh ra-dee
Where can I get . . .	**Gdje mogu dobiti . . .**
	gd-yeh mog-oo dob-eetee . . .
an adaptor for this?	**adapter za ovo?**
	adap-ter za ov-o
a bottle of butane gas?	**bocu plina butana?**
	botsoo pleena boot-ana
a bottle of propane gas?	**bocu plina propana?**
	botsoo pleena prop-an-ah
a fuse?	**električni osigurač?**
	el-ektreechnee oseegoo-rach
an insecticide spray?	**nešto za tamanjenje kukaca?**
	neshto za taman-yen-yeh kook-atsa
a light bulb?	**električnu žarulju?**
	el-ektreechnoo sharool-yoo
The drains are blocked	**Začepio se kanal**
	za-chep-ee-o seh kanal
The sink is blocked	**Začepio se sudoper**
	za-chep-ee-o seh sood-oper
The toilet is blocked	**Začepila se toaleta**
	za-che-pee-la seh twa-leh-ta
The gas is leaking	**Plin propušta**
	pleen prop-oosh-ta

Can you mend it straightaway?	**Možete li ga popraviti odmah?** mosh-et-eh lee ga poprav-eetee odmuh
When can you mend it?	**Kada ga možete popraviti?** ka-dah ga mosh-et-eh poprav-eetee
How much do I owe you?	**Koliko vam dugujem?** kol-eeko vum doog-oo-yem
When is the rubbish collected?	**Kada se kupi smeće?** ka-da seh koopee smeh-cheh

LIKELY REACTIONS

What's your name?	**Vaše ime?** vasheh eemeh
What's your address?	**Koja je vaša adresa?** koya yeh vasha adresa
There's a shop . . .	**Ima dućan** eema doo-chan
in town	**u gradu** oo gra-doo
in the village	**na selu** na seh-loo
I can't come . . .	**Ne mogu doći . . .** neh mog-oo dochee . . .
today	**danas** dan-us
this week	**ove sedmice** ov-eh sedmee-tseh
until Monday	**do ponedjelka** doh poned-yelka
I can come . . .	**Mogu doći . . .** mog-oo dochee . . .
on Tuesday	**u utorak** oo ootorak
when you want	**kad hoćete** kad hoch-et-eh
Every day	**Svaki dan** sva-kee dun
Every other day	**Svaki drugi dan** sva-kee droog-ee dun
On Wednesday	**U srijedu** oo sree-yeh-doo

[*For days of the week, see p. 130*]

General shopping

The drug store/The chemist's

ESSENTIAL INFORMATION

- Look for the words **APOTEKA** or
  LJEKARNA, a large cross or this sign:
- Medicines can also be bought at
  supermarkets or department stores.
- Try the drug store *before* going to a
  doctor: they are usually qualified to
  treat minor injuries.
- Drug stores are normally open between
  8:00 a.m. and 9:00 p.m. However, some 'duty' drug stores are open
  twenty-four hours, look for **DEŽURNA APOTEKA** on the shop
  door or in the local newspaper.
- Some toiletries can also be bought at a **PARFUMERIJA** but they
  will be more expensive.
- Finding a drug store, see p. 20.

WHAT TO SAY

I'd like . . .	**Želio/željela* bih . . .**
	shel-yo shel-yel-ah beeh . . .
some Alka Seltzer	**Alku Seltzer**
	alkoo seltzer
some antiseptic	**antiseptičnu mast**
	anti-septeech-noo must
some aspirin	**aspirinu**
	aspee-ree-noo
some bandage	**zavoj**
	tza-voy
some cotton wool	**vatu**
	va-too
some eye drops	**kapi za oči**
	kap-ee za ochee
some foot powder	**puder**
	pooder

*Men use the first alternative, women the second

some gauze dressing	**gazu**
	ga-zoo
some inhalant	**nešto za udisanje**
	neshto za oodee-san-yeh
some insect repellent	**sredstvo protiv insekata**
	sret-stvo prot-eev insek-ata
some lip salve	**pomadu za usne**
	poma-doo za oosneh
some nose drops	**kapi za nos**
	kap-ee za nos
some sticking plaster	**flaster**
	fluster
some throat pastilles	**tablete za grlo**
	tablet-eh za gher-lo
some Vaseline	**vazelin**
	vazel-in
I'd like something for . . .	**Želio/željela* bih nešto za . . .**
	shel-yo/shel-yel-ah beeh
	neshtoo za . . .
bites	**ubode**
	oobod-eh
burns	**opekotine**
	opek-ot-eeneh
chilblains	**ozebline**
	ozeb-leeneh
a cold	**nahladu**
	na-hladoo
constipation	**tvrdu stolicu**
	tver-doo stol-eetsoo
a cough	**kašalj**
	kash-eye
diarrhoea	**proljev**
	prol-yev
earache	**bol uha**
	bohl ooha
flu	**gripu**
	gree-poo
scalds	**oparenje**
	oparen-yeh
sore gums	**upalu desni**
	oop-aloo deh-snee

*Men use the first alternative, women the second

I'd like something for . . .	**Želio/željela* bih nešto za . . .**
	shel-yo/shel-yel-ah beeh neshtoo za . . .
sprains	**iščašenje**
	ees-chash-en-yeh
stings	**ubode**
	oobod-eh
sunburn	**opeklinu od sunca**
	opek-lee-noo od soon-tsa
travel sickness	**protiv mučnine**
	prot-eev mooch-neen-eh
I need . . .	**Treba/trebaju* mi . . .**
	treb-a/treba-yoo mee . . .
some baby food	**dijećija hrana**
	dee-yech-eeya he-rana
some contraceptives	**kontraceptivno sredstvo**
	kontra-tsep-teev-no sret-stvo
some deodorant	**deodorant**
	deodorant
some disposable nappies	**papirne pelene**
	pap-eer-neh pel-en-eh
some handcream	**krema za ruke**
	krem-a za roo-keh
some lipstick	**ruž za usne**
	roosh za oosneh
some make-up remover	**nešto za čišćenje lica**
	neshto za chee-shen-yeh leetsa
some paper tissues	**papirne maramice**
	pap-eer-neh ma-ram-eetseh
some razor blades	**žilete**
	sheel-et-eh
some safety pins	**pribadača**
	preebada-cha
some sanitary towels	**mjesečne uloške**
	m-yesech-neh oolosh-keh
some shaving cream	**krema za brijanje**
	krem-a za bree-yan-yeh
some soap	**sapun**
	sap-oon
some suntan lotion/oil	**losion/ulje za sunčanje**
	lotion/ool-yeh za soon-chan-yeh

*For singular objects use the first alternative,
    for plural objects use the second

some talcum powder	**talk**
	talc
some Tampax	**Tampax**
	tampax
some (soft) toilet paper	**mekani toaletni papir**
	mek-anee twa-let-nee pap-eer
some toothpaste	**pasta za zube**
	pasta za zoobeh

[*For other essential expressions, see 'Shop talk' p. 56*]

Holiday items

ESSENTIAL INFORMATION

- Places to shop at and signs to look for:
  PAPIRNICA (stationery)
  KNJIŽARA (bookshop)
  FOTO STUDIO (films)
  and main department stores like: **ROBNA KUĆA**
- If you wish to buy local crafts look for the following sign
  NARODNA RADINOST. These shops, to be found in larger
  towns and tourist resorts, specialize in hand-made embroidery,
  filigree jewellery and ceramics.

WHAT TO SAY

Where can I buy . . . ?	**Gdje mogu kupiti . . . ?**
	gd-yeh mog-oo koop-eet-ee . . .
I'd like . . .	**Želio/željela* bih . . .**
	shel-yo/shel-yel-ah beeh . . .
a bag	**torbu**
	torboo
a beach ball	**loptu za plažu**
	lop-too za pla-shoo
a bucket	**kantu**
	kan-to
an English newspaper	**engleske novine**
	en-gleskeh nov-eeneh
some envelopes	**koverta**
	kovair-ta
a guide book	**vodiča**
	vod-eecha
a map (of the area)	**plan okolice**
	plan ok-ol-eetseh
some postcards	**dopisnica**
	doh-pees-neetsa
a spade	**lopatu**
	lop-atoo
a straw hat	**slamnat šešir**
	slam-nat shesheer

*Men use the first alternative, women the second

a suitcase	**kofer**
	kof-fair
some sunglasses	**naočale za sunce**
	na-och-al-eh za soon-tseh
a sunshade	**suncobran**
	soon-tsobran
an umbrella	**kišobran**
	keesh-obran
some writing paper	**papira za pisanje**
	papeera za pee-san-yeh
I'd like . . .	**Želio/željela* bih . . .**
[show the camera]	shel-yo/shel-yel-ah beeh . . .
a colour film	**film u boji**
	film oo boyee
a black and white film	**film crno bijeli**
	film tser-no beeyeh-lee
for prints	**za kopije**
	za kop-ee-yeh
for slides	**za dijapozitiv**
	za deeya-pozitiv
12 (24/36) exposures	**dvanaest (dvadesétčetiri/ tridesetšest) snimaka**
	dva-naest (dva-deh-set chet-eeree/ tree-deh-set-shehst) sneem-akah
a standard film	**standard film**
	standard film
a super 8 film	**super osam**
	soopair o-sam
some flash bulbs	**fleš lampe**
	flash lam-peh
This camera is broken	**Ovaj foto-aparat je pokvaren**
	ov-eye foto-aparat yeh pok-va-ren
The film is stuck	**Film se zaglavio**
	film seh zaglav-ee-o
Please can you . . .	**Molim, možete li . . .**
	mol-im mosh-et-eh lee . . .
develop this?	**razviti ovo?**
	raz-vee-tee ov-o
load the camera for me?	**staviti film u foto-aparat?**
	stav-eetee film oo foto-aparat

[For other essential expressions, see 'Shop talk', p. 56].

*Men use the first alternative, women the second

The smoke shop

ESSENTIAL INFORMATION

- A smoke shop is called **TRAFIKA**. Look also for
  DUHAN — tobacco.
- To ask if there is one near by, see p. 20.
- Nearly all smoke shops sell postage stamps (see p. 100)
- A smoke shop is sometimes part of a stationery store or newsstand.

WHAT TO SAY

A packet of cigarettes **. . .**	**Kutiju cigareta . . .** k*oo*tee-yoo tseega-r*e*h-ta **. . .**
with filters	**sa filterom** sa f*ee*l-tairom
without filters	**bez filtera** bez f*ee*l-taira
king size	**duge** d*oo*g-eh
menthol	**mentol** mentol
Those up there **. . .**	**One tamo gore . . .** *o*n-eh t*a*-mo g*o*reh **. . .**
on the right	**na desno** na d*e*s-no
on the left	**na lijevo** na l*ee*-yeh-vo
These [*point*]	**Ove** *o*v-eh
Cigarettes, please	**Cigarete, molim** tseega-r*e*h-teh m*o*l-im
100, 200, 300	**Sto, dvjesta, trista** sto, dvee-yeh-sta, tr*ee*-sta
Two packets	**Dvije kutije** dv*ee*-yeh k*oo*tee-yeh

Do you have . . .	**Imate li . . .**
	*ee*mat-eh lee . . .
English cigarettes?	**engleskih cigareta?**
	en-gles-keeh tseega-*reh*-ta
American cigarettes?	**amerikanskih cigareta?**
	ameri*kan*-skeeh tseega-*reh*-tah
English pipe tobacco?	**engleskog duhana za lulu?**
	en-gleskog d*oo*-ha-na za l*oo*loo
American pipe tobacco?	**amerikanskog duhana za lulu?**
	american-skog d*oo*-ha-na za l*oo*loo
rolling tobacco?	**duhana za praviti cigarete?**
	d*oo*-ha-na za pra-veetee
	tseega-*reh*-teh
A packet of pipe tobacco	**Paket duhana za lulu**
	p*a*cket d*oo*-ha-na za l*oo*loo
That one up there . . .	**Taj, tamo gore . . .**
	t*a*-ee t*a*-mo g*o*reh . . .
on the right	**na desno**
	na d*e*s-no
on the left	**na lijevo**
	na lee-*yeh*-vo
This one [*point*]	**Ovaj**
	*o*v-aee
A cigar, please	**Cigar, molim**
	ts*ee*-gar m*o*l-im
This one [*point*]	**Ovaj**
	*o*v-aee
Some cigars, please	**Cigara, molim**
	ts*ee*-ga-ra m*o*l-im
Those [*point*]	**Te**
	teh
A box of matches	**Kutiju šibica**
	k*o*otee-yoo sh*ee*-bee-tsa
A packet of pipe cleaners	**Paket čistača za lulu**
	p*a*cket ch*ee*st-acha za l*oo*loo
A packet of flints [*show lighter*]	**Paket kremenova**
	p*a*cket krem-en-ova
Lighter fuel	**Benzin za upaljač**
	ben-z*ee*n za oop*a*l-yach
Lighter gas, please	**plin za upaljač, molim**
	pl*ee*n za oop*a*l-yach m*o*l-im

[*For other essential expressions, see 'Shop talk' p. 56*]

Buying clothes

ESSENTIAL INFORMATION

- Look for:
  ŽENSKA KONFEKCIJA (women's clothes)
  MUŠKA KONFEKCIJA (men's clothes)
  OBUĆA (shoe shop)
- Don't buy without being measured first or without trying things on.
- Don't rely on conversion charts of clothing sizes (see p. 141). If you are buying for someone else, take their measurements with you.

WHAT TO SAY

I'd like . . .	**Želio/željela* bih . . .** shel-yo/shel-yel-ah beeh . . .
an anorak	**vindjaku** wind-yackoo
a belt	**kaiš** ka-ish
a bikini	**bikini** bikini
a bra	**grudnjak** groodn-yak
a cap (swimming)	**kapu (za plivanje)** kap-oo (za pleevan-yeh)
a cap (skiiing)	**kapu (za skijanje)** kap-oo (za ski-yan-yeh)
a cardigan	**kardigan** cardigan
a coat	**kaput** kap-ot
a dress	**haljinu** hal-yee-noo
a hat	**šešir** shesheer
a jacket	**žaket** jacket

*Men use the first alternative, women the second

a jumper	**sviter**	sv*ee*ter
a nightdress	**spavaćicu**	spav*ach*-eetsoo
a pullover	**pulover**	p*u*llover
a raincoat	**kišni kaput**	k*ee*sh-nee k*a*p-oot
a shirt	**košulju**	k*o*sh-ool-yoo
a skirt	**suknju**	s*oo*k-nee-yoo
a suit	**odijelo**	·odee-yel-o
a swimsuit	**kupaći kostim**	k*oo*pachee c*o*stume
a tee-shirt	**majicu**	m*a*-yeetsoo
I'd like . . .	**Želio/željela* bih . . .**	sh*e*l-yo/sh*e*l-yel-ah beeh . . .
a pair of pyjamas	**pidžamu**	peej*a*moo
a pair of shorts	**šorc**	shorts
I'd like a pair of . . .	**Želio/željela* bih par . . .**	sh*e*l-yo/sh*e*l-yel-ah beeh par . . .
briefs (women)	**gaćica**	g*a*ch-eetsa
gloves	**rukavica**	rook*a*v-itsa
jeans	**farmerka**	f*a*rmer-ka
socks	**sokne**	sok-neh
stockings	**čarapa**	ch*a*-rapa
tights	**hulahopke**	h*oo*la-hopkeh
trousers	**pantalona**	pantalona
underpants (men)	**muških gača**	m*oo*sh-keeh g*a*cha

*Men use the first alternative, women the second

I'd like a pair of . . .	**Želio/željela* bih par . . .**
	shel-yo/shel-yel-ah beeh par . . .
shoes	**cipela**
	tsee-pela
canvas shoes	**patika**
	pat-eeka
sandals	**sandala**
	sandala
beach shoes	**cipela za plažu**
	tsee-pela za plashoo
smart shoes	**elegantnih cipela**
	elegant-neeh tsee-pela
boots	**čizama**
	cheezama
moccasins	**mokasinka**
	mokass-inka
My size is . . .	**Moja mjera je . . .**
[For numbers, see p. 125]	moya mee-yaira yeh . . .
Can you measure me, please?	**Možete li uzeti moje mjere, molim?**
	mosh-et-eh lee oozet-ee moyeh mee-yaireh mo-lim
Can I try it on?	**Mogu li da probam?**
	mog-oo lee da pro-bam
It's for a present	**Ovo je za dar**
	ov-o yeh za dah
These are the measurements [show written]	**Ovo su mjere**
	ov-o soo mee-yaireh
bust	**poprsje**
	popers-yeh
chest	**prsa**
	persa
collar	**ovratnik**
	ovrat-neek
hips	**bokovi**
	bockovee
leg	**noga**
	noga
waist	**pas**
	paas

*Men use the first alternative, women the second

Have you got something . . .	**Imate li nešto . . .**
	*ee*mat-eh lee n*e*shto **. . .**
in black?	**u crno?**
	oo ts*e*rno
in white?	**u bijelo?**
	oo bee-y*e*l-**o**
in grey?	**u sivo?**
	oo s*ee*vo
in blue?	**u plavo?**
	oo pl*a*-vo
in brown?	**u smedje?**
	oo sm*e*h-jeh
in pink?	**u roza?**
	oo r*o*dza
in green?	**u zeleno?**
	oo zel*e*h-no
in red?	**u crveno?**
	oo ts*e*r-ven-o
in yellow?	**u žuto?**
	oo sh*oo*-to
in this colour? *[point]*	**u ovoj boji?**
	oo *o*v-oy b*o*yee
in cotton?	**u pamuku?**
	oo p*a*m-ookoo
in denim?	**u traper-platnu?**
	oo tr*a*-per-platnoo
in leather?	**u koži?**
	oo k*o*sh-ee
in nylon?	**u najlonu?**
	oo n*y*lonoo
in suede?	**u jelenoj koži?**
	oo yel-en-oy k*o*sh-ee
in wool?	**u vuni?**
	oo v*oo*nee
in this material? *[point]*	**u ovoj tkanini?**
	oo *o*v-oy t-k*a*n-ee*nee*

[For other essential expressions, see 'Shop talk', p. 56]

*Men use the first alternative, women the second

Replacing equipment

ESSENTIAL INFORMATION

- Look for these shops:
  ŽELJEZARA (hardware)
  ELEKTRIČNI MATERIJAL (electrical goods)
- In a supermarket, look for this display ŽELJEZNARIJA
- To ask the way to the shop, see p. 20
- At a campsite try their shop first, if there is one.

WHAT TO SAY

Have you got . . .	Imate li . . .
	*ee*mat-eh-lee . . .
an adaptor?	**adaptor?**
[*show appliance*]	ad*a*p-tor
a bottle of butane gas?	**bocu butana plina?**
	b*o*tsoo b*oo*t-ana pl*ee*na
a bottle of propane gas?	**bocu propana plina?**
	b*o*tsoo pr*o*p-ana pl*ee*na
a bottle opener?	**vadičep?**
	vad*ee*-chep
any disinfectant?	**sredstvo za dezinfekciju?**
	sr*e*t-stvo za dezeen-f*e*k-tsee-yoo
any disposable cups?	**papirne šalice?**
	p*a*p-eer-neh sh*a*l-eetseh
any disposable plates?	**papirne tanjure?**
	p*a*p-eer-neh tan-y*oo*-reh
a drying up cloth?	**krpu za sušenje?**
	k*e*r-poo za s*oo*-shen-yeh
any forks?	**vilica?**
	v*ee*l-eetsa
a fuse? [*show old one*]	**električni osigurač?**
	e-ektreechnee oseeg*oo*-rach?
an insecticide spray?	**sprej za tamanjenje kukaca?**
	spray za tam*a*n-yen-yeh k*oo*ka-tsa
a kitchen roll? (paper)	**papira za kuhinju?**
	pap*ee*-ra za k*oo*-heen-yoo
any knives?	**noža?**
	n*o*sha

a light bulb	**žarulju?**
[*show old one*]	shar-ool-yoo
a plastic bucket?	**kantu od plastike?**
	kan-too od plast-ee-keh
a plastic can?	**limenku od plastike?**
	leemen-koo od plast-ee-keh
a scouring pad?	**žicu za posudje?**
	sheetsoo za pos-oojeh
a spanner?	**ključ za matice?**,
	klee-yooch za matee-tseh
a sponge?	**spužvu?**
	spoosh-voo
any string?	**špaga?**
	shpa-ga
any tent pegs?	**štipaljke za šator?**
	shteepal-keh za sha-tor
a tin opener?	**otvarač za konzerve?**
	ot-varach za konzair-veh
a torch?	**džepnu lampu**
	jepnoo lampoo
any torch batteries?	**baterije za džepnu lampu?**
	batairee-yeh za jepnoo lampoo
a universal plug (for the sink)?	**univerzalan čep (za pilo)**
	oonivair-zalan chep (za peelo)
a washing line?	**konopac za sušenje rublja?**
	kono-pats za sooshen-yeh roobl-ya
any washing powder?	**prašak za pranje rublja?**
	prashak za pran-yeh roobl-ya
a washing-up brush?	**četku za pranje?**
	chet-koo za pran-yeh
any washing-up liquid?	**tekućinu za pranje sudja?**
	tekooch-eenoo za pran-yeh sood-ya

[*For other essential expressions, see 'Shop talk', p. 56*]

Shop talk

ESSENTIAL INFORMATION

- The currency in Croatia is the Kuna, consisting of 100 smaller units, called Lipa.
  Coins: 1, 2, 5, 10, 20, 50 Lipa
  Notes: 5, 10, 20, 50, 100, 200, 500, 1000 Kuna
- The currency in Yugoslavia is the Yugoslav Dinar, consisting of 100 smaller units, called Para.
  Coins: 10, 20, 50 Para; 1, 2, 5 Dinara.
  Notes: 10, 50, 100, 200, 500, 1000 Dinara.
- Know how to say the important weights and measures:
  [*For numbers, see p. 125*]

50 grams	**Pedeset grama**
	peh-deh-set gra-ma
100 grams	**Sto grama**
	sto gra-ma
200 grams	**Dvjesta grama**
	dvee-yeh-sta gra-ma
½ kilo	**Pola kila**
	pol-a keela
1 kilo	**Kilo**
	keelo
2 kilos	**Dva kila**
	dva keela
½ litre	**Pola litre**
	pol-a leetreh
1 litre	**Litra**
	leetra
2 litres	**Dvije litre**
	dvee-yeh leetreh

- In small shops don't be surprised if customers, as well as the shop assistant, say 'hello' and 'goodbye' to you.

CURRENCY CONVERTER

● Since the relative strengths of currencies vary, it is not possible to provide accurate exchange rates here. However, by filling in the charts below prior to your trip, you can create a handy currency converter.

Kuna	Dollars	Dinar
	1	
	2	
	3	
	4	
	5	
	10	
	15	
	25	
	50	
	75	
	100	
	250	

Kuna	Dollars	Dollars	Dinar
1			1
5			5
10			10
20			20
30			30
40			40
50			50
75			75
100			100
250			250
500			500
750			750
1,000			1,000

CUSTOMER

Hello	**Dobar dan** dob-ar dun
Good morning	**Dobro jutro** dob-ro yootro
Good afternoon	**Dobar dan** dob-ar dun
Goodbye	**Zbogom** zbog-om
I'm just looking	**Samo gledam** sa-mo gled-am
Excuse me	**Oprostite** oprost-eet-eh
How much is this/that?	**Koliko košta ovo/to?** kol-eeko koshta ov-o/toh
What is that?	**Što je to?** shto yeh toh
What are those?	**Što su te?** shto soo teh
Is there a discount?	**Ima li popusta?** eema lee pop-oosta
I'd like that, please	**Želio/željela* bih to molim** shel-yo/shel-yel-ah beeh toh mol-im
Not that	**Ne to** neh toh
Like that	**Onako** on-a-ko
That's enough, thank you	**To je dosta, hvala** toh yeh dosta fa-la
More please	**Više, molim** veesheh mol-im
Less	**Manje od toga** man-yeh od tog-a
That's fine	**To je dobro** toh yeh dob-ro
OK	**Dobro je** dob-ro yeh
I won't take it, thank you	**Neću to, hvala vam** nech-oo toh fa-la vum

*Men use the first alternative, women the second

It's not right	**Nije točno**
	nee-yeh toch-no
Thank you very much	**Velika vam hvala**
	vel-eeka vum fa-la
Have you got something . . .	**Imate li nešto . . .**
	eemat-eh lee neshto . . .
better?	**bolje?**
	bol-yeh
cheaper?	**jevtinije?**
	yeft-een-yeh
different?	**različitije?**
	razleech-eet-yeh
larger?	**veće?**
	veh-cheh
smaller?	**manje?**
	man-yeh
At what time do you . . .	**U koliko sati . . .**
	oo kol-eeko sa-tee . . .
open?	**otvarate?**
	otvara-teh
close?	**zatvarate?**
	zatvara-teh
Can I have a bag, please?	**Mogu li da dobijem kesicu, molim?**
	mog-oo lee da dob-ee-yem kes-eetsoo mol-im
Can I have a receipt?	**Mogu li da dobijem priznanicu?**
	mog-oo lee da dob-ee-yem preeznan-eetsoo
Do you take . . .	**Primate li . . .**
	preemat-eh lee . . .
English/American money?	**engleski/amerikanski novac?**
	en-gleskee/amerikan-skee nov-ats
travellers' cheques?	**putne čekove?**
	poot-neh check-oveh
credit cards?	**Kreditne karte?**
	cred-eetneh karteh
I'd like . . .	**Želio/željela* bih . . .**
	shel-yo/shel-yel-ah beeh . . .
one like that	**jedan kao taj**
	yed-an kow ta-ee
two like that	**dva kao ti**
	dva kow teeh

*Men use the first alternative, women the second

SHOP ASSISTANT

Can I help you?	**Mogu li vam pomoći?**
	mog-oo lee vum pom-ochee
What would you like?	**Što želite?**
	shto shel-eeteh
Is that all?	**Je li to sve?**
	yeh lee toh sveh
Anything else?	**Nešto drugo?**
	neshto droogo
Would you like it wrapped?	**Želite li da vam zamotam?**
	shel-eeteh lee da vum zamot-an
Sorry, none left	**žao mi je nemamo više**
	sha-o mee yeh nem-amo veesheh
I haven't got any	**Nemam ni jedan**
	nem-am nee yed-an
I haven't got any more	**Nemam više**
	nem-am veesheh
How many do you want?	**Koliko ih želite?**
	kol-eeko shel-eeteh
Is that enough?	**Je li to dosta?**
	yeh lee toh dosta?

Shopping for food

Bread

ESSENTIAL INFORMATION

- Finding a baker's, see p. 20
- Key words to look for:
  PRODAVAONICA KRUHA
  PEKARNA
  TRGOVINA KRUHA
- Mini-markets, supermarkets of any size and general stores nearly always sell bread.
- Opening times: 7.00/7.30 a.m. – 12.00 p.m. and 5.00 p.m. – 8.00 p.m. Saturday: 7.00/7.30 a.m. to 12.00 p.m.
- The most characteristic type of loaves in Croatia are **pogača** which are large, flat and round. However, the words for the various types of bread differ throughout Yugoslavia and you should be prepared to point to what you want.

WHAT TO SAY

Some bread, please	**Kruha, molim**
	kr*oo*ha m*o*l-im
One loaf (like that)	**Jednu pogaču (kao tu)**
	yed-noo p*o*g-achoo (kow too)
A large one	**Veliku**
	vel-eekoo
A small one	**Malu**
	m*a*l-oo
One bread roll	**Jednu rusicu**
	yed-noo r*oo*-see-tsoo
.250 grams of . . .	**Dvjesta pedeset grama . . .**
	dvee-yeh-sta peh-deh-set gr*a*-ma . . .
½ kilo of . . .	**Pola kile . . .**
	p*o*l-a k*ee*leh . . .
1 kilo of . . .	**Kilo . . .**
	k*ee*lo . . .
bread	**kruha**
	kr*oo*ha

1 kilo of . . .	**Kilo . . .** keelo . . .
white bread	**bijelog kruha** bee-yel-og krooha
wholemeal bread	**crnog kruha** tser-nog krooha
bread rolls	**rusica** roo-see-tsa
Two loaves	**Dvije pogače** dvee-yeh pog-acheħ
Four bread rolls	**Četiri rusice** chet-eeree roo-see-tsch

[*For other essential expressions, see 'Shop talk', p. 56*]

Cakes

ESSENTIAL INFORMATION

- Key word to look for:
  SLASTIČARNA (cake shop)
- To find a cake shop, see p. 20.
- **KAVANA** is a place where cakes can be bought to be eaten on the premises or taken away – alcoholic drinks are also served.
- Ordering a drink, see p. 80.

WHAT TO SAY

The type of cakes you find in the shops varies from region to region but the following are some of the most common.

doboš torta doh-bosh torta	chocolate layer cake with glazed sugar topping
hladna krema ladna krem-a	custard pie
krafen kraf-en	doughnut
krem pita krem peeta	custard cake
išler eesh-ler	éclair

marcapan
martsapaŋ

marzipan

pita od jabuka
peeta od ya-booka

apple strudel

pita od sira
peeta od seera

cheese cake

princes krafne
princes kraf-neh

cream doughnut

trokut
trok-oot

mille feuilles

šampita
shampeeta

tart with whipped cream and
    meringue mixture

You usually buy medium-size cakes by number:

One doughnut	**Jedan krafen** yed-an kraf-en
Two doughnuts, please	**Dva krafena, molim** dva kraf-en-a mol-im

You buy small cakes by weight:

200 grams of biscuits	**Dvjesta grama keksa** dvee-yeh-sta gra-ma kex-ah
400 grams of petit fours	**Četrsto grama kolačića** chet-ersto gra-ma kolach-ee-cha

You may want to buy a larger cake by the slice:

One slice of apple cake	**Jedan komad štrudela** yed-an kom-ad shtrood-la
Two slices of almond cake	**Dva komada torte od badema** dva kom-a-da torteh od ba-dem-a

You may also want to say:

A selection, please	**Miješanih, molim** mee-yesh-aneeh mol-im

[*For other essential expressions, see 'Shop talk', p. 56*]

Ice-cream and sweets

ESSENTIAL INFORMATION

- Key words to look for:
  SLADOLED (ice cream)
  SLASTIČARNA (cake shop)
- Prepacked sweets are available in general stores, supermarkets and ice-cream stalls in the streets. There is no Yugoslav equivalent of a sweet shop.

WHAT TO SAY

A . . . ice, please	**Sladoled . . . molim** sla-doh-led . . . mol-im
banana	**od banana** od banan-a
chocolate	**od čokolade** od chokola-deh
hazelnut	**od lješnjaka** od l-yeh-shen-yaka
raspberry	**od malina** od ma-leena
strawberry	**od jagoda** od ya-goda
vanilla	**od vanilje** od vaneel-yeh
A single	**Jedan** yed-an
Two singles	**Dva** dva
A double	**Jedan dupli** yed-an doop-lee
Two doubles	**Dva dupla** dva doopla
A cone	**Kornet** kor-net

A packet of . . .	**Paket . . .**
	pack-et
100 grams of . . .	**Sto grama . . .**
	sto gra-ma . . .
200 grams of . . .	**Dvjesta grama . . .**
	dvee-yeh-sta gra-ma . . .
sweets	**slatkiša**
	slat-keesha
toffees	**štolvera**
	shtol-vera
chocolates	**čokolade**
	chokola-deh
mints	**mentina**
	menteena
A lollipop	**Lilihipa**
	lilly-heep

[For other essential expressions, see 'Shop talk' p. 56]

In the supermarket

ESSENTIAL INFORMATION

- The place to ask for:
  ROBNA KUĆA (department store)
  SUPERMARKET
  MINIMARKET
  ŽIVEŽNE NAMIRNICE (general food store)
- Key instructions on signs in the shop:
  ULAZ (entrance)
  ZABRANJEN ULAZ (no entry)
  IZLAZ (exit)
  ZABRANJEN IZLAZ (no exit)
  NEMA IZLAZA (no way out)
  BLAGAJNA (cash desk)
  PONUDE (on offer)
  SAMOPOSLUGA (self-service)
- Most supermarkets are open throughout the day during the week and on Saturday mornings. Some self-service shops also open on Sunday mornings.
- No need to say anything in a supermarket, but ask if you can't see what you want.

WHAT TO SAY

Excuse me, please	**Izvinite, molim Vas**
	eez-veen-eeteh mol-im vus
Where is . . .	**Gdje je . . .**
	gd-yeh yeh . . .
the bread?	**kruh?**
	krooh
the butter?	**maslac?**
	mas-laːs
the cheese?	**sir?**
	seer
the chocolate?	**čokolada?**
	chokola-da
the coffee?	**kava?**
	ka-va

the cooking oil?	**ulje za kuhanje?**
	ool-yeh za koo-han-yeh
the frozen food?	**zaledjena hrana?**
	zalej-en-a hrah-na
the fruit?	**voće?**
	vocheh
the fruit juice?	**voćni sok?**
	voch-nee soak
the jam?	**djem?**
	jam
the meat?	**meso?**
	meh-so
the milk?	**mlijeko?**
	mlee-yek-o
the mineral water?	**mineralna voda?**
	meenairal-na vod-a
the pasta?	**pasta?**
	pasta
the salt?	**sol?**
	sol
the sugar?	**šećer?**
	shecher
the tea?	**čaj?**
	cha-ee
the tinned fish?	**konzervirana riba**
	konzairv-eekana reeba
the tinned fruit?	**konzervirano voće**
	konzairv-eekano vocheh
the vegetable section?	**povrće?**
	pov-ercheh
the vinegar?	**ocat?**
	ots-at
the wine?	**vino?**
	veeno
the yogurt?	**yogurt?**
	yogourt
Where are . . .	**Gdje su . . .**
	gd-yeh soo . . .
the biscuits?	**keksi?**
	kex-ee
the crisps?	**krisps?**
	crisps

Where are . . .	Gdje su . . .
	gd-yeh soo . . .
the eggs?	**jaja?**
	ya-ya
the seafoods?	**morski školjkari?**
	mors-kee shkol-karee
the snails?	**puži**
	poo-shee
the soft drinks?	**nealkoholna pića?**
	nehalkohol-na peechah
the sweets?	**slatkiši**
	slat-keeshee
the tinned vegetables?	**konzervirano povrće?**
	konzairv-eerano pov-ercheh

[*For other essential expressions, see 'Shop talk', p. 56*]

Picnic food

ESSENTIAL INFORMATION

- Key words to look for:
  DELIKATESNA RADNJA (delicatessen)
  MESARNICA (butcher's)
  ŽIVEŽNE NAMIRNICE (grocer's)
- Weight guide:
  4–6 oz/150 g of prepared salad per two people, if eaten as a starter
  to a substantial meal.
  3–4 oz/100 g of prepared salad per person, if to be eaten as the
  main part of a picnic-style meal.

WHAT TO SAY

One slice of . . .	**Jedan odrezak . . .**
	yed-an od-rez-ak . . .
Two slices of . . .	**Dva odreska**
	dva od-res-ka . . .
roast beef	**govedjeg pečenja**
	gov-ed-yeg pech-en-ya
roast pork.	**svinjskog pečenja**
	sveen-skog pech-en-ya
tongue	**jezika**
	yez-eeka
ham	**šunke**
	shoonkeh
paté	**paštete**
	pash-teh-teh
garlic sausage	**kobasica**
	kobas-eetsah
salami	**salame**
	salam-eh
100 grams of . . .	**Sto grama . . .**
	sto gra-ma . . .
150 grams of . . .	**Sto pedeset grama . . .**
	sto peh-deh-set gra-ma . . .
200 grams of . . .	**Dvjesta grama . . .**
	dvee-yeh-sta gra-ma

300 grams of . . .	**Trista grama . . .**
	tree-sta gra-ma
russian salad	**ruske salate**
	roosk-eh sal-at-eh
tomato salad	**salate of paradajza**
	sal-at-eh od parada-ee za
beetroot salad	**salate od cikle**
	sal-at-eh od tseek-leh
mixed salad	**mješane salate**
	m-yeshan-eh sal-at-eh
carrot salad	**salate od mrkve**
	sal-at-eh od merk-veh
green salad	**salate zelene**
	sal-at-eh zel-en-eh
olives	**maslina**
	musleena
anchovies	**inćuna**
	eenchoona
cheese	**sira**
	seera

You might also like to try some of these:

dalmatinski pršut	ham from Dalmatia
dalmat-eenskee per-shoot	
dimljeni sir	smoked cheese
diml-yen-ee seer	
domaće kobasice	homemade sausages
domacheh kobas-eetseh	
domaći sir	local cheese
domachee seer	
jastog	lobster
yast-og	
kajmak	rich soft cheese made from scalded
ka-eemuk	milk
kamenice	oysters
kamen-eetseh	
kranjske kobasice	sausages from Slovenia
kran-yes-keh kobas-eetseh	
kuhana šunka	cooked ham
koohana shoon-ka	
marinirana riba	marinated fish
marin-eerana reeba	

mliječni sir	milk cheese
mlee-*vech*-nee seer	
pašteta od džigerice	liver paté
pash-*teh*-ta od *jeeg*-eritseh	
pašteta od mesa	meat paté
pash-*teh*-ta od *meh*-sa	
paški sir	cheese from Pag island
pash-kee seer	
pečena guska	roast goose
pech-ena *goo*ska	
pečena patka	roast duck
pech-ena *patka*	
pečeno pile	roast chicken
pech-eno *peeleh*	
pečena teletina	roast veal
pech-ena *teh*-leh-teena	
pohano meso	fried meat in breadcrumbs
po-hano *meh*-soh	
pohano pile	fried chicken in breadcrumbs
po-hano *peeleh*	
punjena jaja	stuffed eggs
poon-yen-ah *ya*-ya	
sardine	sardines
sardeeneh	
sir sa vrhnjem	curd cheese with sour cream
seer sa *verhen*-yem	
sušene haringe	smoked herrings
sooshen-eh *har*-een-gheh	
trapist	ewe's milk cheese (firm and mild)
trap-eest	
tunjevina	tuna fish
toon-*yev*-eena	

[*For other essential expressions, see 'Shop talk', p. 56*]

Fruit and vegetables

ESSENTIAL INFORMATION

- Key words to look for:
  VOĆE (fruit)
  VOĆARNA (fruit shop)
  POVRĆE (vegetables)
- If possible, buy fruit and vegetables in the market where they are cheaper and fresher than in the shops. Open air markets are held in most areas.
- It is customary for you to choose your own fruit and vegetables at the market (and in some shops) and for the stallholder to weigh and price them. You must take your own shopping bag: paper and plastic bags are not normally provided.
- Weight guide: 1 kilo of potatoes is sufficient for six people for one meal.

WHAT TO SAY

½ kilo (1 lb) of . . .	**Pola kila . . .** pol-ah keela . . .
1 kilo of . . .	**Kilo . . .** keelo . . .
2 kilos of . . .	**Dva kila . . .** dva keela . . .
apples	**jabuka** ya-booka
apricots	**marelica** mar-el-eetsa
bananas	**banana** banana
cherries	**trešanja** treshan-ya
figs	**smokve** smok-veh
grapes (white/black)	**grožđja (bijeloga/crnoga)** grosh-ja (bee-yeloga/tsernoga)
oranges	**naranača** naran-acha
pears	**krušaka** kroosha-ka

peaches	**breskava**
	bresk-ava
plums	**šljiva**
	shl-*ee*va
strawberries	**jagoda**
	y*a*-goda
A pineapple, please	**Ananas, molim**
	*a*nanas m*o*l-im
A grapefruit	**Grejpfrut**
	gr*a*pefruit
A melon	**Dinju**
	d*ee*n-yoo
A water melon	**Lubenicu**
	loob*e*n-eetsoo
250 grams of . . .	**Dvjesta pedeset grama . . .**
	dvee-yeh-sta peh-d*e*h-set gr*a*-ma . . .
½ kilo of . . .	**Pola kila . . .**
	p*o*l-a k*ee*la . . .
1 kilo of . . .	**Kilo . . .**
	k*ee*lo . . .
1½ kilos of . . .	**Kilo i po . . .**
	k*ee*lo ee p*o* . . .
2 kilos of . . .	**Dva kila . . .**
	dv*a*h k*ee*la . . .
aubergines	**melancane**
	melan-tsaneh
beans	**graha**
	gr*a*-ha
carrots	**mrkve**
	m*e*rk-veh
courgettes	**tikvice**
	t*ee*k-veetseh
green beans	**mahuna**
	mah*oo*-na
leeks	**poriluka**
	por*ee*l-ooka
mushrooms	**gljiva**
	gl*ee*va
onions	**luka**
	l*oo*ka
peas	**graška**
	gr*a*shka
potatoes	**krompira**
	kr*o*mp-eera

2 kilos of . . .	**Dva kila . . .**
	dv*a*h k*ee*la . . .
spinach	**spanaća**
	span*a*cha
tomatoes	**paradajza**
	parad*a*-eeza
A bunch of . . .	**Kitu . . .**
	k*ee*too . . .
parsley	**peršuna**
	persh-*oo*na
radishes	**rotkvica**
	rot-kvee-tsa
A head of garlic	**Glava češnjaka**
	gl*a*va cheshn-y*a*-ka
A lettuce	**Salata**
	s*a*l-ata
A cauliflower	**Karfiol**
	karf*ee*-ol
A cabbage	**Kupus glavati**
	k*oo*poos gl*a*v-atee
A cucumber	**Krastavac**
	kr*a*s-tavats
A turnip	**Repa**
	r*e*p-a
Like that, please	**Tako, molim vas**
	t*a*k-o m*o*l-im vus

Fruit and vegetables which may not be familiar:

blitva
bl*ee*tva
beet leaf: like a large stalky spinach leaf

nešpola
nesh-pol-ah
medlar: small, slightly sour fruit, orange colour, juicy

šipak
sh*ee*pak
pomegranate

višnja
v*ee*shneeya
morello cherry

žučenica
sh*oo*chen-eetsa
young dandelion leaf, used in salads

[*For other essential information, see 'Shop talk' p. 56*]

Meat

ESSENTIAL INFORMATION

- Key words to look for:
  MESARNICA or **MESNICA** (butcher's)
  MESAR (butcher)
- Weight guide: 4-6 ozs/125–200 g of meat per person for one meal.
- The meat is not displayed in the same way as in the UK, nor should you expect to find the same cuts. However, you should tell the butcher whether you intend to boil, to grill or to roast the meat so that he will know what to give you.

WHAT TO SAY

For a joint, choose the type of meat and then say how many people it is for and how you intend to cook it:

Some beef, please	**Komad govedine, molim**
	kom-ad gov-ed-eeneh mol-im
Some lamb	**Komad janjetine**
	kom-ad yan-yet-eeneh
Some mutton	**Komad ovčetine**
	kom-ad ov-chet-eeneh
Some pork	**Komad svinjetine**
	kom-ad sveen-yet-eeneh
Some veal	**Komad teletine**
	kom-ad teh-leh-teeneh
A joint . . .	**Komad . . .**
	kom-ad . . .
for two people	**za dvije osobe**
	za dvee-yeh os-obeh
for four people	**za četiri osobe**
	za chet-eeree os-obeh
for six people	**za šest osoba**
	za shehst os-oba
to boil	**za kuhati**
	za koo-hat-ee
to grill	**za na roštilju**
	za nah rosh-teel-yoo
to roast	**za peći**

For steak, liver or kidneys, do as above

Some steak, please	**Biftek, molim**
	beeftek mol-im
Some liver	**Jetre**
	yet-reh
Some kidneys	**Bubrega**
	boob-reg-ah
Some sausages	**Kobasice**
	kobas-eetseh
for three people	**za tri osobe**
	za tree os-obeh
for five people	**za pet osoba**
	za pet os-obah

For chops do it this way:

Two veal escalopes, please	**Dvije teleće šnicle, molim**
	dvee-yeh teh-lech-eh shniits-leh mol-im
Three pork chops	**Tri svinjska kotleta**
	tree sveen-ska kot-leh-ta
Four mutton chops	**Četiri ovčja kotleta**
	chet-eeree ov-chee-ya kot-leh-ta
Five lamb chops	**Pet janjećih kotleta**
	peht yan-yech-eeh kot-leh-ta

You may also want:

A chicken	**Pile**
	peeleh
A rabbit	**Kunić**
	koonich
A tongue	**Jezik**
	yez-eek

Other essential expressions [*see also p. 56*]

Please can you . . .	**Molim vas možete li . . .**
	mol-im vus mosh-et-eh lee . . .
mince it?	**faširati?**
	fash-eer-atee
dice it?	**izrezati na kocke?**
	eezrez-atee na kots-keh
trim the fat?	**otkinuti debelo?**
	otkee-noo-tee deb-el-oh

Fish

ESSENTIAL INFORMATION

- The place to ask for: **RIBARNICA** (fishmonger's)
- Markets usually have fish stalls.
- Weight guide: 8 oz/250 g minimum per person for one meal of fish bought on the bone.
  i.e. ½ kilo/500 g   for two people
       1 kilo   for four people
       1½ kilos   for six people
- It is not normal practice in Yugoslavia for the fishmonger to fillet fish, and you may also find that some fishmongers will not clean fish, so check beforehand.

WHAT TO SAY

Purchase large fish and small shellfish by weight:

½ kilo of . . .	**Pola kila . . .**
	pol-a keela . . .
1 kilo of . . .	**Kilo . . .**
	keelo . . .
1½ kilos of . . .	**Kilo i po . . .**
	keelo ee po . . .
bass	**brancina**
	bran-tseena
carp	**šarana**
	shar-ana
squid	**liganja**
	leegan-ya
cod (dried)	**bakalara**
	bakalar-ah
cod (fresh)	**svježog bakalara**
	svye-shog bakalar-ah
eels	**jegulja**
	yeg-ool-ya
grey mullet	**cipola**
	tseep-ola
lobster	**jastoga**
	yas-tog-ah

1½ kilos of . . .	**Kilo i po . . .**
	keelo ee po . . .
mussels	**mušula**
	moosh-oola
oysters	**kamenica**
	kamen-eetsa
prawns	**gambora**
	gambora
red mullet	**barbuna**
	barboona
scampi	**škampija**
	shkam-peea
sole	**listova**
	leestova
pilchards	**sardela**
	sard-ela

Some large fish can be purchased by the slice:

One slice of . . .	**Komad . . .**
	kom-ad . . .
Two slices of . . .	**Dva komada . . .**
	dva kom-a-da . . .
Six slices of . . .	**Šest komada . . .**
	shehst kom-a-da . . .
salmon	**lososa**
	los-os-a
cod	**bakalara**
	bakalar-a
fresh tuna	**tunjevine**
	toon-jev-eeneh

For some shellfish and 'frying pan' fish, say the name and then specify the number you want [*For numbers, see p. 125*]

A crab	**Rak**
	rak mol-im
A lobster	**Jastog**
	yas£tog
A whiting	**Merlan**
	mair-lan
An ink fish	**Sipa**
	seepa

An octopus	**Hobotnica**
	*h*ob-otneetsah
A sole	**List**
	leest
A trout	**Pastrva**
	p*a*st-erva
A mackerel	**Lokarda**
	l*o*k-arda
A herring	**Haringa**
	h*a*r-eenga
A pike	**Štuka**
	sht*oo*ka
A carp	**Šaran**
	sh*a*r-an

Other essential expressions [*see also p. 56*]

Please can you . . .	**Molim vas možete li . . .**
	m*o*l-im vus mosh-et-eh lee . . .
take the heads off?	**otkinuti glave?**
	*o*t-kee-noo-tee gl*a*-veh
clean them?	**očistiti ih?**
	*o*cheest-eetee

Eating and drinking out

Ordering a drink

ESSENTIAL INFORMATION

- The place to ask for: **KAVANA** (see p. 20)
- By law, the price list of drinks must be displayed outside or in the window.
- There is waiter service in all cafés, but you can drink at the bar or counter if you wish (cheaper).
- Always leave a tip of 10%-15% of the bill unless you see **SERVIS UKLJUČEN** (service included) printed on the bill or on a notice.
- Cafés serve non-alcoholic drinks and alcoholic drinks, and are normally open all day. Children may accompany their parents into bars.
- Local mineral water is available.
- The following list of drinks are all local brandies which you may like to try: **kajsjevača** (apricot brandy), **komovica** (brandy made from grape-pressings), **orahovica** (brandy made from grape pressings with green shells of walnuts in it), **rakija** (brandy from fruit pressings), **šljivovica** (plum brandy).

WHAT TO SAY

I'll have . . .	**Htio/htjela* bih . . .** ht*ee*-o/ht-y*e*lah beeh . . .
a black coffee	**crnu kavu** ts*er*-noo k*a*-voo
a coffee with cream	**kavu sa šlagom** k*a*-voo sa shl*a*g-om
a tea	**čaj** ch*a*-ee
with milk	**sa mlijekom** sa mlee-yek-om
with lemon	**sa limunom** sa l*ee*moon-om
a glass of milk	**čašu mlijeka** ch*a*sh-oo mlee-y*e*k-*a*
two glasses of milk	**dvije čaše mlijeka** dv*ee*-yeh ch*a*sh-eh mlee-y*e*k-*a*

*Men use the first alternative, women the second

a hot chocolate	**kakao**
	kak*a*-o
a mineral water	**mineralnu vodu**
	m*ee*nairal-noo v*o*d-oo
a lemonade	**limunadu**
	leem*oo*n*a*-doo
a lemon squash	**sok limuna**
	s*oa*k leem*oo*na
a Coca Cola	**koka-kolu**
	c*o*ca-c*o*loo
an orangeade	**oranžadu**
	or*a*nj*a*-doo
an orange juice	**sok od naranče**
	s*oa*k od n*a*ran-cheh
a grape juice	**sok od grožđja**
	s*oa*k od gr*o*sh-ja
a pineapple juice	**sok od ananasa**
	s*oa*k od *a*nanasa
a small bottle of beer	**malu bocu pive**
	m*a*-loo b*o*tsoo p*ee*veh
a large bottle of beer	**veliku bocu pive**
	v*e*l-eekoo b*o*tsoo p*ee*veh
A glass of . . .	**Čašu . . .**
	ch*a*sh-oo . . .
Two glasses of . . .	**Dvije čaše . . .**
	dv*ee*-yeh ch*a*sh-eh . . .
red wine	**crnog vina**
	ts*e*r-nog v*ee*na
white wine	**bijelog vina**
	bee-y*e*l-og v*ee*na
rosé wine	**ružičastog vina**
	r*oo*sh-chast-og v*ee*na
sparkling wine	**pjenušava vina**
	pee-y*e*n-oosh-ava v*ee*na
champagne	**šampanjca**
	shamp*a*ntsa
A whisky . . .	**Viski . . .**
	v*i*skey . . .
with ice	**sa ledom**
	sa l*e*d-om
with water	**sa vodom**
	sa v*o*d-om
with soda	**sa sodom**
	sa s*o*d-om

A gin . . .	**Džin . . .** gin . . .
and tonic	**sa tonikom** sa tonic-om
with lemon	**sa limunom** sa leemoon-om
A brandy/cognac	**Konjak** cognac

[*For the names of typical Yugoslav brandies, see 'Essential information' above*]

Other essential expressions:

Miss! [*This does not sound abrupt in Serbo-Croat*]	**Gospodjice!** gospoj-yeetseh
Waiter!	**Konobar!** kon-obar
The bill, please	**Račun molim** rach-oon mol-im
How much does that come to?	**Koliko je to?** kol-eeko yeh toh
Is service included?	**Da li je servis uračunat?** da lee yeh sair-vis oorach-oonat
Where is the toilet, please?	**Gdje je toaleta, molim?** gd-yeh yeh twa-leh-ta mol-im

Ordering a snack

ESSENTIAL INFORMATION

- Look for a café or bar with these signs:
  BAR
  BIFE (snack bar)
  GRILL
- Look for the names of snacks (listed below) on signs in the window.
- In some regions mobile vans sell hot snacks.
- For cakes, see p. 62.
- For ice-cream, see p. 64.
- For picnic-type snacks, see p. 69.

WHAT TO SAY

I'll have . . . please	**Molim vas htio/htjela* bih . . .**
	mol-im vus htee-o/ht-yelah beeh . . .
a cheese sandwich	**sendvič od sira**
	send-wich od seera
a ham sandwich	**sendvič od šunke**
	send-wich od shoonkeh
a pancake	**palačinku**
	palach-inkoo
a packet of crisps	**paketić krispsa**
	pack-et-ich krisp-sa

These are some other snacks you may like to try:

sendvič od budžole	a pork sausage sandwich – **a**
send-wich od boojol-eh	speciality
sendvič od čajne kobasice	a sandwich of smoked sausage
send-wich od chaee-neh	
kobas-eetseh	
sendvič od dalmatinske šunke	a Parma ham sandwich
send-wich od dalmat-eenskeh	
shoonkeh	
sendvič od Gavrilović salame	a salami sandwich (Gavrilovic is
send-wich od gavril-ovich	Yugoslavia's best known salami)
sala-meh	

*Men use the first alternative, women the second

sendvič od gušče pastete   a goose paté sandwich
send-wich od goosh-cheh
  pash-tet-eh
sendvič od livanskog sira   a Serbian cheese sandwich
send-wich od leevan-skog seera
sendvič od mortadele   a mortadella sandwich
send-wich od mortadel-eh
sendvič od piletine   a chicken sandwich
send-wich od peelet-eeneh

Chips are not available as snacks. They can only be ordered as
part of a meal in a restaurant when you should ask for **'pom frit'.**
[*For other essential expressions, see 'Ordering a drink', p. 80*]

In a restaurant

ESSENTIAL INFORMATION

- The place to ask for:
  RESTORAN [*see p. 20*]
  You can eat at these places:
  RESTORAN
  BIFE
  (light snacks, alcoholic and soft drinks)
  EKSPRES RESTORAN
  (self-service, available only in large towns)
  GOSTIONA
  (modest restaurant)
  KAVANA
  (ice-creams, cakes, tea, coffee and alcoholic drinks)
  MLIJEČNI RESTORAN
  (dairy bar)
  RIBLJI RESTORAN
  (principally for fish dishes)

- By law, the menus must be displayed outside or in the window:
  and that is the *only* way to judge if a place is right for your needs.

- Self-service restaurants do exist, but most places have waiter service.

- Tipping is not obligatory but even where service is included, it is customary to tip 10% of the bill.

- Children's portions (**POLA PORCIJE**) are not commonly available, but it may be worth asking.

- Eating times are flexible and vary between 12.00 p.m. to 13.00 p.m. and 7.00 p.m. to 11.00 p.m.

WHAT TO SAY

May I book a table?	**Mogu li rezervirati jedan stol?**
	mog-oo lee rezair-veer-atee yed-an stol
I've booked a table	**Imam rezervirani stol**
	eem-um rezair-veer-anee stol
A table . . .	**Stol . . .**
	stol . . .
for one	**za jedno**
	za yed-no
for three	**za troje**
	za troy-eh
The menu, please	**Jelovnik, molim**
	yelov-neek mol-im
The fixed-price menu	**Pansionski jelovnik**
	pansion-skee yelov-neek
The tourist menu	**Turistički jelovnik**
	toorist-ich-kee yelov-neek
Today's special menu .	**Današnji specijalni jelovnik**
	dan-ashn-yee spetsial-nee yelov-neek
What's this, please? [*point to the menu*]	**Što je ovo, molim?**
	shto yeh ov-o mol-im
The wine list	**Vinska karta**
	veen-ska karta
A carafe of wine, please	**Bocu vina, molim**
	botsoo veena mol-im
A quarter (25 cc)	**Četvrt litre vina**
	chet-vert leetreh veena
A half (50 cc)	**Pola litre vina**
	pol-a leetreh veena
A glass	**Čašu**
	cha-shoo
A bottle	**Bocu**
	botsoo
A half-bottle	**Pola boce**
	pol-a botseh
A litre	**Litru**
	leet-roo
Red/white/rosé/house wine	**Crnog/bijelog/ružičastog/domaćeg vina**
	tser-nog/bee-yel-og/roosh-ichastog/ domach-eg veena

Some more bread, please	**Malo više kruha, molim** ma-lo veesheh krooha, mol-im
Some more wine	**Malo više vina** ma-lo veesheh veena
Some oil	**Malo ulja** ma-lo ool-ya
Some vinegar	**Malo octa** ma-lo ots-ta
Some salt	**Malo soli** ma-lo sol-ee
Some pepper	**Malo bibera** ma-lo beeb-era
Some water	**Malo vode** ma-lo vod-eh
How much does that come to?	**Koliko to košta?** kol-eeko to koshta
Is service included?	**Da li je servis uračunat?** da lee yeh sait-vis oorach-oonat
Where is the toilet, please?	**Gdje je toaleta, molim?** gd-yeh yeh twa-leh-ta, mol-im
Miss! [*This does not sound abrupt in Serbo-Croat*]	**Gospodjice!** gospoj-yeetseh
Waiter!	**Konobar!** kon-obar
The bill, please	**Račun, molim** rach-oon mol-im

Key words for courses, as seen on some menus
[*Only ask the question if you want the waiter to remind you of the choice.*]

What have you got in the way of . . .	**Što imate za . . .** shto eemat-eh za . . .
STARTERS?	**PREDJELO?** pred-ee-yelo
SOUP?	**JUHU?** yoo-hoo
EGG DISHES?	**JAJA?** ya-ya
FISH?	**RIBU?** reeboo
MEAT?	**MESO?** meh-so

GAME?	**DIVLJAČ?**
	deev-leeach
FOWL?	**PILETINU?**
	peelet-eenoo
VEGETABLES?	**POVRĆE?**
	pov-ercheh
CHEESE?	**SIR?**
	seer
FRUIT?	**VOĆE?**
	voch-eh
ICE-CREAM?	**SLADOLED**
	sladoh-led
DESSERT?	**DEZERT?**
	dezairt

UNDERSTANDING THE MENU

- You will find that most menus in Yugoslavia are in one or more European languages and the names of the various dishes will differ all over the country.
- You will find the names of the principal ingredients of most dishes on these pages:

  Starters see p.69   Fruit see p. 72
  Meat see p. 75   Dessert see p. 62
  Fish see p. 77   Cheese see p. 69
  Vegetables see p. 73   Ice-cream see p. 64

- Used together with the following list of cooking and menu terms, they should help you to decode the menu.
- These cooking and menu terms are for understanding only – not for speaking aloud.

Cooking and menu terms

banjo marija	bain marie
na dalmatinsku	Dalmatian
dimljeno	smoked
dinstovano	stewed
dobro kuvano⎤	well done
dobro pečeno ⎦	
faširano	minced
filovano	stuffed
frigano	fried

garnirano	garnished
na gradele	grilled
gusta juha	thick soup
hladno	cold
juha	broth
sa kiselim vrhnjem	with sour cream
kuvano	boiled
kuvano u pari	steamed
na maslu	with butter
meso u hladetini	meat in aspic jelly
minestrun	vegetable soup
mljeveno	ground
sa mušulama	with mussels
pasirano	creamed
u peć	in the oven
pečeno	roast
pirjano (podušeno)	poached
pire	purée
polupečeno	rare
u prosulju	in the frying pan
punjeno	stuffed
na puteru	with butter
prženo	fried
ragu	stew
na ražnju	on the spit
na roštilju	grilled
seckano	diced
slatko/kiselo	sweet/sour
srednje pečeno	medium done
ukiseljeno (meso/riba)	marinated (meat/fish)
u umaku	with sauce
na žaru	grilled on charcoal

Further words to help you understand the menu

bakalar	cod (dried)
barbuni	red mullet
bubrezi	kidneys
ćevapčići	kebab of minced meat
djuveč	a vegetable dish of tomatoes with peppers and aubergines, sometimes part of a meat stew – the menu will specify

dvopek u kremi	trifle
faširano meso	minced meat
fazan	pheasant
file steak	fillet steak
gavuni	sprats
girice	small Adriatic fish (sprats)
golub	pigeon
govedje pečenje	roast beef
janjeće pečenje	roast lamb
jarebica	partridge
jastog	lobster
jegulje	eels
jetra	liver
jezik	tongue
juha od paradajza	tomato soup
kobasice	sausages
kolač	cake
krezle	sweetbreads
kunić	rabbit
lignji	squid
marinirane gljive	marinated mushrooms
mozak	brain
musaka	moussaka: layers of minced meat and sliced aubergines with a topping of eggs and sour milk.
omleti	omelets
palačinke	pancakes
patka	duck
piletina na ražnju	chicken on the spit
piletina pržena	fried chicken
piletina pohana	chicken fried in breadcrumbs
punjena jaja	stuffed eggs
punjeni patlidžan	stuffed aubergines
punjeni paradajz	stuffed tomatoes
punjene paprike	stuffed peppers in tomato sauce
punjene tikvice	stuffed courgettes
puran	turkey
rak	crab
razne salate	various salads
razni sladoledi	various ice-creams
ražnjici	pieces of pork/veal on skewers → shish kebab

riblja juha	fish soup
rižot	risotto
salama	salami
sarma	stuffed and pickled cabbage leaves in tomato sauce
škampi na žaru	scampi grilled on charcoal
slanina	bacon
srce	heart
šunka	ham
svinjska glava	pig's head
svinjska koljenica	pig's trotters
svinjsko pečenje	roast pork
teleće pečenje	roast veal
zelena menestra	green leaf soup with ham
zec (divlji)	hare (wild)
zubatac	a large delicately flavoured fish (dentex)

Health

ESSENTIAL INFORMATION

- For details of reciprocal health agreements between your country and the country you are visiting, visit your local Department of Health office at least one month before leaving, or ask your travel agent.
- It is, however, also advisable to purchase a medical insurance policy through a travel agent, a broker or a motoring organization.
- Take your own 'first line' first aid kit with you.
- For minor disorders and treatment at a drugstore, see p. 42.
- For finding your way to a doctor, dentist and drug store, see p. 20.
- Once in Yugoslavia decide on a definite plan of action in case of serious illness: communicate your problem to a near neighbour, the receptionist or someone you see regularly. You are then dependent on that person helping you obtain treatment.

WHAT'S THE MATTER?

I have a pain in my . . .	Boli me . . .
	bol-ee meh . . .
ankle	**članak**
	chlan-ak
arm	**ruka**
	rooka
back	**ledja**
	lej-ah
bladder	**mjehur**
	m-yeh-hoor
bowels	**crijeva**
	tsree-yeh-va
breast	**grudi**
	groodee
chest	**prsa**
	per-sa
ear	**uho**
	oo-ho
eye	**oko**
	o-ko

foot	**stopalo**
	stop-alo
head	**glava**
	gla-va
heel	**peta**
	peh-ta
jaw	**vilica**
	veelee-tsa
kidney	**bubreg**
	boob-reg
leg	**noga**
	nog-a
lungs	**pluća**
	plooch-ah
neck	**vrat**
	ver-at
penis	**penis**
	peh-nis
shoulder	**rame**
	ra-meh
stomach (abdomen)	**stomak**
	stomach
testicle	**mudo**
	moodo
throat	**grlo**
	ger-lo
vagina	**vagina**
	vag-eena
wrist	**ručni zglavak**
	rooch-nee z-glav-ak
I have a pain here [*point*]	**Boli me ovdje**
	bol-ee meh ovd-yeh
I have toothache	**Boli me zub**
	bol-ee meh zoob
I have broken . . .	**Slomio/slomila* sam . . .**
	slom-ee-o/slom-eela sum . . .
my dentures	**moju protezu**
	moyoo protez-oo
my glasses	**moje naočale**
	moyeh now-cha-leh

*Men use the first alternative, women the second

I have lost . . .	**Izgubio/izgubila* sam . . .** *eez*-goobee-o/*eez*-goobee-la sum . . .
my contact lenses	**moja kontaktna stakla** m*o*ya c*o*ntact-na st*a*k-la
a filling	**plombu** pl*o*m-boo
My child is ill	**Moje je dijete bolesno** m*o*yeh yeh dee-*y*et-eh b*o*l-esno
He/she has a pain in his/her . . .	**Boli ga/boli je . . .** b*o*l-ee ga/b*o*l-ee yeh . . .
ankle [*see list above*]	**članak** chl*a*n-ak

How bad is it?

I'm ill	**Ja se osjećam bolestan/bolesna*** ya seh *o*s-yech-am b*o*l-estan/ b*o*l-esna
It's urgent	**Hitno je** h*ee*t-no yeh
It's serious	**Ozbiljno je** *o*z-beel-no yeh
It's not serious	**Nije ozbiljno** n*ee*-yeh *o*z-beel-no
It hurts	**Boli** b*o*l-ee
It hurts a lot	**Boli puno** b*o*l-ee p*oo*no
It doesn't hurt much	**Ne boli puno** neh b*o*l-ee p*oo*no
The pain occurs . . .	**Bol se ponavlja redovito . . .** bohl seh pon-avl-ya red*o*v-eeto . . .
every quarter of an hour	**svako četvrt sata** sv*a*k-o ch*e*tvert s*a*-ta
every half an hour	**svako pola sata** sv*a*k-o p*o*l-a s*a*-ta
every hour	**svaki sat** sv*a*k-ee s*a*ht
every day	**svaki dan** sv*a*k-ee d*u*n
most of the time	**većinom vremena** vech*ee*n-om vr*e*m-ena

*Men use the first alternative, women the second

I've had it for . . .	**Boli me već ima . . .** bol-ee meh vech eema . . .
one hour/one day	**jedan sat/jedan dan** yed-an saht/yed-an dun
two hours/two days	**dva sata/dva dana** dva sa-ta/dva da-na
It's a . . .	**To je . . .** toh yeh . . .
sharp pain	**jaka bol** yak-a bohl
dull ache	**mrtva bol** mert-va bohl
nagging pain	**uporna bol** oopor-na bohl
I feel dizzy	**Vrti mi se u glavi** ver-tee mee seh oo gla-vee
I feel sick	**Zlo mi je** zlo mee yeh
I feel weak	**Slabo mi je** sla-bo mee yeh
I feel feverish	**Grozničav sam** groz-neechav sum

Already under treatment for something else?

I take . . . regularly [show]	**Uzimum redovito . . .** oozee-mum redov-eetoh . . .
this medicine	**ovaj lijek** ov-oy lee-yek
these pills	**ove pilule** ov-eh peelool-eh
I have . . .	**Bolujem od . . .** boloo-yem od . . .
a heart condition	**srca** ser-tsa
haemorrhoids	**hemoroida** hem-oroyda
rheumatism	**reumatizma** reh-oomat-eezma

I am . . .	**Ja sam . . .** ya sum . . .
diabetic	**dijabetičar** dee-*a*-bet-eechar
asthmatic	**astmatičar** asm*a*t-eechar
pregnant	**očekujem bebu** *o*chek-ooyem b*e*b-oo
I'm allergic to penicillin	**Ja sam alergičan/alergična* na penicilin** ya sum *a*lairg-ichan/*a*lairg-ich-na na penitsil-*ee*noo

Other essential expressions

Please can you help?	**Molim, možete li pomoći?** m*o*l-im m*o*sh-et-eh lee p*o*m-ochee
A doctor, please	**Doktora, molim** d*o*ctora m*o*l-im
A dentist	**Zubara** z*oo*bara
I don't speak Serbo-Croat	**Ne govorim srpsko-hrvatski** neh g*o*v-orim serpsko-h*e*rvatskee
What time does . . .	**U koliko sati . . .** oo k*o*l-eeko s*a*-tee . . .
the doctor open?	**doktor počimje raditi?** d*o*ctor poch*ee*m-yeh r*a*d-eetee
the dentist open?	**zubar počimje raditi?** z*oo*bar poch*ee*m-yeh r*a*d-eetee

From the doctor: key sentences to understand

Take this . . .	**Uzmite ovo . . .** *oo*z-meet-eh *o*v-o . . .
every day/hour	**svaki dan/svaki sat** sv*a*k-ee d*a*n/sv*a*k-ee s*a*ht
Stay in bed	**Ostanite u krevetu** *o*stan-eet-eh oo kr*e*v-et-oo
Don't travel . . .	**Nemoj te putovati . . .** nem-oy teh poot*o*v-atee . . .
for . . . days/weeks	**za . . . dana/sedmice** za . . . d*a*-na/s*e*d-mee-tseh
You must go to hospital	**Treba da idete u bolnicu** tr*e*b-a da *ee*d-et-eh oo b*o*lnee-tsoo

*Men use the first alternative, women the second

Problems: complaints, loss, theft

ESSENTIAL INFORMATION

- Problems with:
  camping facilities, see p. 36
  household appliances, see p. 38
  health, see p. 92
  the car, see p. 106
- If the worst comes to the worst, find the police station. To ask the way, see p. 20.
- Look for:
  MILICIJA (police)
  SAOBRAĆAJNA MILICIJA (traffic police)
  POGRANIČNA MILICIJA (frontier police)
  LUČKA KAPETANIJA (port authority)
- If you lose your passport, go to your nearest consulate.
- In an emergency dial 94 for an ambulance, 93 for the fire brigade and 92 for the police.

COMPLAINTS

I bought this . . .
Kupio sam ovo . . .
k*oo*pee-o sum *ov*-o . . .

today
danas
d*a*-nus

yesterday
juČer
y*oo*ch-er

on Monday [*see p. 130*]
u ponedjeljak
oo pon-*e*d-yel-yak

It's no good
Nije dobro
n*ee*-yeh d*o*b-ro

Look
Pogledajte
p*o*gleh-daee-teh

Here [*point*]
Ovdje
*o*vd-yeh

Can you . . .
Možete li . . .
m*o*sh-et-eh lee . . .

change it?
promijenuti?
promee-y*e*n-ootee

mend it?
popraviti?
p*o*prav-eetee

Here's the receipt	**Ovdje je priznanica** _ovd_-yeh yeh preeznan-eetsa
Can I have a refund?	**Mogu li dobiti novac natrag?** m_og_-oo lee d_ob_-eetee n_ovats_ n_ah_trag
Can I see the manager?	**Mogu li da vidim direktora?** m_og_-oo lee da v_ee_deem deerect_o_ra

Loss
[See also 'Theft' below: the lists are interchangeable]

I have lost . . .	**Izgubio/izgubila sam*** . . . _eez_-goobee-o/_eez_-goobee-la sum . . .
my bag	**moju tašnu** m_oy_oo t_a_shnoo
my bracelet	**moju narukvicu** m_oy_oo na-rook-veetsoo
my camera	**moj fotoaparat** moy photo-_a_parat
my car keys	**ključeve mojih kola** klee-y_oo_ch-eh-veh m_oy_eeh kola
my car logbook	**saobraćajnu knjižicu** sa-_o_bracha-eenoo kn-y_ee_-shee-tsoo
my driving licence	**moju vozačku dozvolu** moy-oo vozach-koo d_o_z-vol-oo
my insurance certificate	**moju potvrdu osiguranja** moy-oo p_ot_-ver-doo oseegoo-r_a_n-yah
my jewellery	**moje dragulje** m_oy_-eh drag-_oo_l-yeh
everything	**sve** sveh

Theft
[See also 'Loss' above: the lists are interchangeable]

Someone has stolen . . .	**Ukrali su mi . . .** _oo_kra-lee soo mee . . .
my car	**moja kola** moya kola
my car radio	**radio mojih kola** ra-dio m_oy_eeh kola

*Men use the first alternative, women the second

my money	**moj novac**
	moy nov-ats
my necklace	**moju ogrlicu**
	moy-oo og-erlee-tsoo
my passport	**moj pasoš**
	moy pas-osh
my radio	**moj radio**
	moy ra-dio
my tickets	**moje karte**
	moy-eh karteh
my travellers' cheques	**moje putne čekove**
	moy-eh poot-neh chek-oveh
my wallet	**moj novčanik**
	moy nov-chan-ik
my watch	**moj sat**
	moy saht
my luggage	**moju prtljagu**
	moy-oo pertl-ya-goo

LIKELY REACTIONS: key words to understand

Wait	**Počekajte**
	poch-ek-ah-eeteh
When?	**Kada?**
	ka-da
Where?	**Gdje?**
	gd-yeh
Name?	**Ime?**
	eemeh
Address?	**Adresa?**
	adresa
I can't help you	**Ne mogu vam pomoći**
	neh mog-oo vum pom-ochee
Nothing to do with me	**To nije moja stvar**
	toh nee-yeh moya stvar

The post office

ESSENTIAL INFORMATION

- To find a post office, see p. 20.
- Key words to look for **POŠTA, TELEGRAF I TELEFON**
- Look for this sign:

- For stamps look for the word **MARKE** on a post office counter.
- Stamps are also sold at smoke shops, newsstands, and stationery stores.
- Letter boxes are yellow, and fixed to the walls.
- For post-restante, you should show your passport at the counter marked **POST RESTANTE:** a small fee is usually payable.

WHAT TO SAY

To England, please   **Za Englesku, molim**
                                    za en-gles-koo mol-im
[Hand letters, cards or parcels over the counter]
To Australia   **Za Australiju**
                                    za *ah*-oostralee-yoo

To the United States   **za Ameriku**
[For other countries see p. 134] za amerik-oo

How much is . . .	**Koliko košta . . .** kol-eeko koshta . . .
this parcel (to Canada)?	**ovaj paket (za Kanadu)?** ov-aee pack-et (za kanadoo)
a letter (to Australia)?	**pismo (za Australiju)?** peesmo (za ah-oostralee-yoo)
a postcard (to England)?	**dopisnica (za Englesku)?** dop-eesneetsa (za en-gles-koo)
Airmail	**Avionom** avee-onom
Surface mail	**Običnom poštom** obeech-nom posh-tom
One stamp, please	**Jednu marku, molim** yed-noo markoo mol-im
Two stamps	**Dvije marke** dvee-yeh markeh
One (2) dinar stamp	**Jednu marku od (dva) dinara** yed-noo markoo od (dva) deena-ra
I'd like to send a telegram	**Želim da pošaljem telegram** shel-im da poshal-yem telegram

Telephoning

ESSENTIAL INFORMATION

- Unless you read and speak Serbo-Croat well, it's best not to make phone calls by yourself. Go to a post office and write the town and number you want on a piece of paper. Add 'COLLECT CALL' if you want a person-to-person call or PCV if you want to reverse the charges.
- Telephones are usually attached to the walls of public buildings in rectangular brick red boxes – these are for local calls only. Insert the dinar coins as required in the correct slot and dial when the red light appears. Speak when you hear your caller. If you don't get through press down the receiver cradle to recover your money.
- The code for the UK is 9944 followed by the UK subscriber's own telephone number. Calls to the USA have to go through the operator.
- You can ask at your local post office for a brochure on phoning England from abroad.

WHAT TO SAY

Where can I make a telephone call?	**Gdje mogu da telefoniram?**
	gd-yeh mog-oo da telephon-eeram
Local/abroad	**Za unutrašnjost/inozemstvo**
	za oonoo-trashn-yost/eenozems-tvo
I'd like this number . . .	**Želim ovaj broj . . .**
[*show number*]	shel-im ov-eey broy . . .
in England	**za Englesku**
	za en-gles-koo
in Canada	**za Kanadu**
	za kanadoo
in the USA	**za Ameriku**
[*For other countries, p. 134*]	za omerikoo
Can you dial it for me, please?	**Možete li vi nazvati za mene, molim?**
	mosh-et-eh lee vee naz-va-tee za meh-neh mol-im
How much is it?	**Koliko košta?**
	kol-eeko koshta

Hello

Halo/molim
ha-lo/mol-im

May I speak to . . .?

Mogu li govoriti sa . . . ?
mog-oo lee gov-oree-tee sa . . .

Extension . . .

Lokal . . .
local . . .

I'm sorry, I don't speak
  Serbo-Croat

**Žao mi je, ali ne govorim
  srpsko-hrvatski**
sha-o mee yeh ah-lee neh gov-oreem
  serpsko-hervatskee

Do you speak English?

Govorite li vi engleski?
gov-oree-teh lee vee en-gleskee

Thank you, I'll phone back

Hvala, nazvat ću kasnije
fa-la naz-vat choo kasnee-yeh

Goodbye

Zbogom
zbog-om

LIKELY REACTIONS

That's 10 dinars

To košta sto pedeset dinara
to koshta sto peh-deh-set deen-ara

Cabin number (3)
[*For numbers, see p. 125*]
Don't hang up

Govornica broj (tri)
govor-neetsa broy (tree)
Nemojte prekinuti
nem-oy-teh prek-eenoo-tee

I'm trying to connect you

Pokušavam da vas spojim
pokoosh-avum da vus spoy-im

You're through

Imate vezu
eema-teh vez-oo

There's a delay

Ima zakašnjenja
eema zakashnee-yen-ya

I'll try again

Pokušat ću kasnije ponovo
pokoosh-at choo kasnee-yeh
  po-no-vo

Changing checks and money

ESSENTIAL INFORMATION

- Finding your way to a bank or change bureau, see p. 20.
- Look for these words on buildings:
  BANKA (bank)
  MJENJAČNICA (money changed)
  NARODNA BANKA (national bank)
  TURISTIČKA AGENCIJA (most travel agencies will change money)
- Money can also be changed at some post offices. It is illegal to change foreign currency other than in official exchange offices. Avoid all approaches to change money—particularly on trains.
- To cash your own normal checks, exactly as at home, use your credit card where you see the Eurocheque sign. Write in English.
- Have your passport handy.

WHAT TO SAY

I'd like to cash . . .	**Želim da promjenim . . .**
	shel-im da prom-yen-im . . .
this travellers' cheque	**ovaj putni ček**
	ov-aee poot-nee check
these travellers' cheques	**ove putne čekove**
	ov-eh poot-neh check-oveh
this cheque	**ovaj ček**
	ov-aee check
I'd like to change this into dinars	**Želim da promjenim ovo u dinare**
	shel-im da prom-yen-im ov-o oo deen-areh
Here's . . .	**Izvolite . . .**
	eez-vol-eeteh . . .
my banker's card	**moju bankarsku potvrdu**
	moy-oo bankar-skoo pot-ver-doo
my passport	**moj pasoš**
	moy pas-osh

For excursions into neighbouring countries

I'd like to change this . . .	**Želim da promjenim ovo . . .**
[*show banknotes*]	shel-im da prom-yen-im ov-o . . .
into Austrian schillings	**u austrijske šilinge**
	oo ah-oos-tree-skeh shee-leen-geh
into Hungarian forint	**u madžarske forinte**
	oo mad-jar-skeh foreen-teh
into Rumanian leu	**u rumunjske leje**
	oo roomoon-skeh leh-yeh
into Bulgarian lev	**u bugarske leve**
	oo boogar-skeh lev-eh
into Italian lira	**u talijanske lire**
	oo talee-yan-skeh leereh
into Greek drachma	**u grčke drahme**
	oo gerch-keh dra-hmeh
into Albanian lek	**u albanske leke**
	oo alban-skeh lek-eh
What's the rate of exchange?	**Kakav je kurs?**
	ka-kav yeh koors

LIKELY REACTIONS

Passport, please	**Pasoš, molim**
	pas-osh mol-im
Sign here	**Potpišite se ovdje**
	pot-peesh-eeteh seh ovd-yeh
Your banker's card, please	**Vašu bankarsku potvrdu, molim**
	vashoo bankar-skoo pot-ver-doo
	mol-im
Go to the cash desk	**Izvolite na kasu**
	eez-vol-eeteh na ka-soo

Car travel

ESSENTIAL INFORMATION

- Finding a filling station or garage, see p. 20.
- Grades of gasoline:
  NORMAL (86 octane)
  MJEŠAVINA (mixed)
  SUPER (98 octane)
  NAFTA/DIZL (gas oil/diesel)
- 1 gallon is about 4½ litres (accurate enough up to 6 gallons).
- For general repairs, look for the sign
  AUTOMEHANIKA
  Other garages with the proprietor's name in front of the sign
  SERVIS undertake general repair work.
- Opening times: 6.00 a.m. – 12.00 p.m.
- You will find 24-hour service stations along the main roads.
- The Yugoslav Automobile Association (**AMSJ**) runs some 120 assistance/information bases which are manned by mechanics and open between 8.00 a.m. and 8.00 p.m. Some of these stations still have individual telephone numbers, but many of them can be contacted on 987.
- Members of foreign motoring and touring clubs may get free legal advice from lawyers associated with the Yugoslav AA (particularly applicable in larger towns).
- Unfamiliar road signs and warnings, see p. 121.

WHAT TO SAY
[*For numbers, see p. 125*]

(9) litres of . . .	(**Devet**) **litara . . .** deh-vet leet-ara . . .
(150) dinars of . . .	(**Sto pedeset**) **dinara . . .** sto peh-deh-set deen-ara . . .
standard	**normala** normal-ah
premium	**supera** sooper-ah
diesel	**mješavine/nafte** mee-yesha-veeneh/nafteh
Fill it up, please	**Napunite, molim** napoo-neeteh mol-im

Will you check . . .	**Molim vas provjerite . . .** mol-im vus prov-yair-eeteh . . .
the oil?	**ulje?** ool-yeh
the battery?	**akumulator?** akoomoola-tor
the radiator?	**radijator?** rad-ya-tor
the tyres?	**gume?** goomeh
I've run out of petrol	**Ostao sam bez benzine** osta-o sum bez benzeeneh
Can I borrow a can, please?	**Možete li mi posuditi kantu, molim** mosh-et-eh lee mee pos-oodeet-ee kantoo mol-im
My car has broken down	**Kola su mi se pokvarila** kola soo mee seh pok-var-eela
My car won't start	**Ne mogu da pokrenem kola** neh mog-oo da pokreh-nem kola
I've had an accident	**Dogodila mi se nesreća** do-go-dee-la mee seh nes-recha
I've lost my car keys	**Izgubio sam ključeve od kola** eez-goobee-o sum klee-yoo-cheh-veh od kola
My car is . . .	**moja su kola . . .** moya soo kola . . .
two kilometres away	**na dva kilometra odavle** na dva keelo-met-ra od-av-leh
three kilometres away	**na tri kilometra odavle** na tree keelo-met-ra od-av-leh
Can you help me, please?	**Možete li mi pomoći, molim vas?** mosh-et-eh lee mee pom-ochee mol-im vus
Do you do repairs?	**Da li pravite popravke?** da lee pra-veeteh pop-rav-keh
I have a puncture	**Imam probušenu gumu** eem-am pro-booshenoo goomoo
I have a broken windscreen	**Imam razbijeno predje staklo** eem-am raz-bee-yen-o pred-yeh staklo
I think the problem is here . . . [*point*]	**Mislim da je problem ovdje . . .** meeslim da yeh problem ovd-yeh . . .

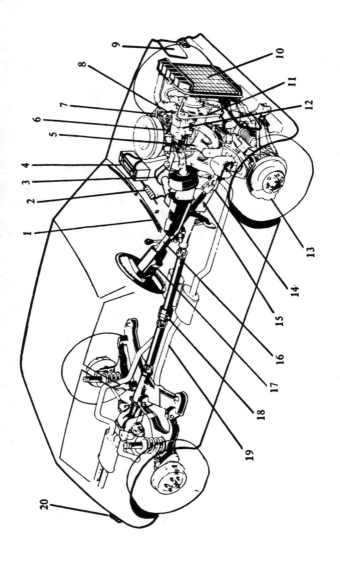

1 windscreen wipers	**brisači**	
	breesach-ee	
2 fuses	**osigurači**	
	oseegoo-rachee	
3 heater	**grijač**	
	gree-yach	
4 battery	**akumulator**	
	akoomoola-tor	
5 engine	**motor**	
	mo-tor	
6 fuel pump	**pumpa benzina**	
	poompa benzeeneh	
7 starter motor	**startni motor**	
	start-nee mo-tor	
8 carburettor	**karburator**	
	kar-boora-tor.	
9 lights	**fare**	
	fa-reh	
10 radiator	**radijator**	
	radee-ya-tor	
11 fan belt	**remen ventilatora**	
	reh-men venteela-tora	
12 generator	**generator**	
	ghenerat-or	
13 brakes	**kočnica**	
	koch-nee-tsa	
14 clutch	**mjenjač**	
	mee-yen-yach	
15 gear box	**kutija mjenjača**	
	kootee-ya m-yen-ya-cha	
16 steering	**upravljanje**	
	oopravl-yan-yeh	
17 ignition	**paljenje**	
	pal-yen-yeh	
18 transmission	**prenos**	
	preh-nos	
19 exhaust	**ispusna cijev**	
	ees-poos-na tsee-yev	
20 indicators	**žmigavci**	
	shmeeg-av-tsee	

I don't know what's wrong	**Ne znam što nije u redu** neh znum shto neeyeh oo red-oo
Can you . . .	**Možete li vi . . .** mosh-et-eh lee vee . . .
repair the fault?	**popraviti kvar?** pop-rav-eetee kvar
come and look?	**doći i pogledati?** doh-chee ee pogleh-da-tee
estimate the cost?	**procijeniti?** pro-tsee-yeh-neetee
write it down?	**napisati?** napees-atee
Do you accept these coupons?	**Da li primate ove kupone?** da lee preemat-eh ov-eh coupon-eh
How long will the repair take?	**Koliko će trebati vremena za popravak?** kol-eeko cheh treb-atee vrem-ena za pop-ra-vak
When will the car be ready?	**Kada će kola biti gotova?** ka-da cheh kola beetee got-ov-ah
Can I see the bill?	**Mogu li da vidim račun?** mog-oo lee da veedeem rach-oon
This is my insurance document	**Ovo je moja isprava osiguranja** ov-o yeh moya eesp-rava oseegooran-ya

HIRING A CAR

Can I hire a car?	**Mogu li da iznajmim kola?** mog-oo lee da eez-naee-mim kola
I need a car . . .	**Trebaju mi kola . . .** treb-ayoo mee kola . . .
for two people	**za dvije osobe** za dvee-yeh os-obeh
for five people	**za pet osoba** za pet os-oba
for one day	**za jedan dan** za yed-an dun
for five days	**za pet dana** za pet dun-ah
for a week	**za jednu nedjelju** za yed-noo ned-yel-yoo

Can you write down . . .
mosh-et-eh lee napees-atee . . ,

the deposit to pay?
Možete li napisati . . .
kolika je kaucija?
kol-eeka yeh cow-tsee-ya

the charge per kilometre?
koliko košta po kilometru?
kol-eeko koshta po keelo-metroo

the daily charge?
koliko košta na dan?
kol-eeko koshta na dun

the cost of insurance?
koliko košta osiguranje?
kol-eeko koshta oseegoo-ran-yeh

Can I leave it in (Split)?
Mogu li da ih ostavim (Split)?
mog-oo lee da ee osta-veem
(spleet)

What documents do I need?
Koji dokumenti su mi potrebni?
koyee doh-koo-mentee soo mee
pot-reb-nee

LIKELY REACTIONS

I don't do repairs
Ne vršim popravke
neh ver-sheem poprav-keh

Where is your car?
Gdje su vaša kola?
gd-yeh soo vasha kola

What make is it?
Koja je marka Vaših kola?
koya yeh marka vash-eeh kola

Come back tomorrow/on
Monday
[*For days of the week, p. 130*]
Povratite se sutra/u ponedjeljak
pov-rat-eeteh seh sootra/oo
poned-yel-yak

I don't hire cars
Ne iznajmivam kola
neh eez-naee-meev-am kola

Your driving licence, please
Vašu vozačku dozvolu, molim
vash-oo voz-ach-koo dozvol-oo

The mileage is unlimited
Kilometraža je neograničena
keelo-metrash-ah yeh neh
neh-ogran-eechena

Public tranport

ESSENTIAL INFORMATION

- Finding the way to the bus station, a bus stop, a trolley stop, the railway station and a taxi stand, see p. 20.
- Remember that lining up for buses is unheard of.
- You can hail a taxi as you would normally but it's best to go to a taxi stand.
- Types of train:
  brzi vlak (stops at principal stations)
  expresni vlak (stops at principal stations; a supplement is payable)
  putnički vlak (stops at all stations)
  poslovni vlak (commuter train)
- Key words on signs [see also p. 121]
  ZELJEZNIČKA STANICA (railway station)
  PRODAJA KARTA (tickets, ticket office)
  ULAZ (entrance)
  ZABRANJENO JE (forbidden)
  ULAZ (entrance, for buses)
  PERON (platform)
  URED ZA INFORMACIJE (information, information office)
  ČEKAONICA (waiting room)
  ŽTP JŽ (initials for Yugoslav railways)
  IZLAZ (exit)
  GARDEROBA (left luggage)
  AUTOBUSNA STANICA (bus stop)
  RED VOŽNJE (timetable)

WHAT TO SAY

Where does the train for (Belgrade) leave from?	**Odakle polazi vlak za (Beograd)?** od-akleh pol-azee vlak za (beh-ograd)
At what time does the train leave for (Belgrade)?	**U koliko sati polazi vlak za Beograd?** oo kol-eeko sa-tee pol-azee vlak za (beh-ograd)
At what time does the train arrive in (Belgrade)?	**U koliko sati stiže vlak u (Beograd)?** oo kol-eeko sa-tee steesh-eh vlak oo (beh-ograd)
[For times, see p. 128]	

Is this train for (Belgrade)?	**Da li je ovo vlak za (Beograd)?**
	da lee yeh ov-o vlak za (beh-ograd)?
Where does the bus for (Split) leave from?	**Odakle polazi autobus za (Split)?**
	od-akleh pol-azee ah-ooto-boos za (spleet)?
At what time does the bus leave for (Split)?	**U koliko sati polazi autobus za (Split)?**
	oo kol-eeko sa-tee pol-azee ah-ooto-boos za (spleet)?
At what time does the bus arrive at (Split)?	**U koliko sati stiže autobus u (Split)?**
	oo kol-eeko sa-tee stee-sheh ah-ooto-boos oo (spleet)?
Is this the bus for (Split)?	**Da li je ovo autobus za (Split)?**
	da lee yeh ov-o ah-ooto-boos za (spleet)?
Do I have to change?	**Moram li da presjedim?**
	mor-am lee da pres-yeh-dim
Where does . . . leave from?	**Odakle polazi**
	od-akleh pol-azee . . .
the bus	**autobus**
	ah-ooto-boos
the train	**vlak**
	vlak
the underground	**podzemna željeznica**
	pod-zem-na shel-yeznee-tsa
for the airport	**za aerodrom**
	za ah-airodrom
for the cathedral	**za katedralu**
	za kat-edral-oo
for the beach	**za plažu**
	za plash-oo
for the market place	**za trg**
	za terg
for the railway station	**željezničku stanicu**
	shel-yez-neech-koo stan-eetsoo
for the town centre	**za centar grada**
	za tsen-tar grad-a
for the St Blase church	**za crkvu Svetog Vlaha**
	za tserk-voo svet-og vla-ha
for the swimming pool	**za bazen**
	za baz-eb

Is this . . .	**Da li je ovo . . .** da lee yeh ov-o . . .
the bus for the market place?	**autobus za trg** ah-ooto-boos za terg
the tram for the railway station?	**tramvaj za željezničku stanicu** tram-vaee za shel-yez-neech-koo stan-eetsoo
Where can I get a taxi?	**Gdje mogu uzeti taksi?** gd-yeh mog-oo oozet-ee taxi?
Can you put me off at the right stop, please?	**Hoćete li mi reći kad treba da se iskrcam, molim vas?** hoch-et-eh lee mee rech-ee kad treb-ah da seh is-ker-tsam mol-im vus
Can I book a seat?	**Mogu li rezervirati jedno mjesto?** mog-oo lee rezairv-eer-atee yed-no m-yesto
A single	**Jednosmjernu kartu** yed-no-smee-yair-noo kartoo
A return	**Jednu povratnu kartu** yed-noo povrat-noo kartoo
First class	**Prvi razred** per-vee raz-red
Second class	**Drugi razred** droo-ghee raz-red
One adult	**Za jednu osobu** za yed-noo os-oboo
Two adults	**Za dvije osobe** za dvee-yeh os-obeh
and one child	**i jedno dijete** ee yed-no dee-yet-eh
and two children	**i dvoje djece** ee dvoyeh dee-yetseh
How much is it?	**Koliko košta?** kol-eeko koshta

LIKELY REACTIONS

Over there	**Tamo** t*a*-mo
Here	**Ovdje** *o*vd-yeh
Platform (1)	**Peron broj (jedan)** p*e*h-ron br*o*y (yed-an)
At 16.00 [*For times, see p. 128*] Change at (Sarajevo)	**U šesnaest** oo sh*e*hst-na-est **Presjedajte u (Sarajevu)** pres-yed-aeeteh oo (s*a*rayevoo)
Change at (the town hall)	**Presjedajte (kod gradske općine)** pres-yed-aeeteh (kod gr*a*t-skeh *o*p-cheeneh)
This is your stop	**Ovo je vaša stanica** *o*v-o yeh v*a*sha stan-eetsa
There's only first class	**Ima samo prvi razred** *ee*ma s*a*-mo per-vee r*a*z-red
There's a supplement	**Ima dodatak** *ee*ma dod*a*t-ak

Leisure

ESSENTIAL INFORMATION

- Finding the way to a place of entertainment, see p. 20.
- For times of day see p. 128.
- Important signs, see p. 121.

WHAT TO SAY

At what time does . . . open?	**U koliko sati se otvara . . .** oo kol-eeko sa-tee seh otva-ra . . .
the art gallery	**umjetnička galerija?** oom-yet-neech-ka galaireeya
the botanical garden	**botanički vrt?** bot-aneech-kee vert
the cinema	**kino?** keeno
the concert hall	**koncertna dvorana?** kontsairt-na dvora-na
the disco	**disko?** disko
the museum	**muzej?** mooz-ay
the night club	**noćni lokal?** noch-nee lok-al
the sports stadium	**stadion?** sta-dee-on
the swimming pool	**bazen?** baz-en
the theatre	**pozorište?** poz-orish-teh
the zoo	**zoološki vrt?** zool-osh-kee vert
At what time does . . . close?	**U koliko sati se zatvara . . .** oo kol-eeko sa-tee seh zatva-ra . . .
the art gallery [see above list]	**umjetnička galerija?** oom-yet-neech-ka galaireeya

At what time does . . . start?	**Kada počimje . . .** ka-da pocheem-yeh . . .
the cabaret	**kabaret?** kabaret
the concert	**koncert?** kon-tsairt
the film	**film?** film
the match	**utakmica?** ootak-meetsa
the play	**drama?** drama
the race	**trka?** ter-ka
How much is it . . .	**Koliko košta . . .** kol-eeko koshta . . .
for an adult?	**za osobu?** za os-oboo
for a child?	**za dijete?** za dee-yet-eh
Two adults, please	**Dvije osobe, molim** dvee-yeh os-obeh mol-im
Three children, please [*State price, if there's a choice*] Stalls/circle	**Troje djece, molim** tro-yeh dee-yet-seh mol-im **Parter/balkon** par-tair/balkon
Do you have . . .	**Imate li . . .** eemat-eh lee . . .
a programme?	**program?** pro-gram
a guide book?	**vodiča?** vod-eecha
Where's the toilet, please?	**Gdje je toaleta, molim?** gd-yeh yeh twa-leh-ta mol-im
Where's the cloakroom?	**Gdje je garderoba?** gd-yeh yeh gardeh-roba
I'd like lessons in . . .	**Želio/željela* bih lekcije . . .** shel-yo/shel-yel-ah beeh lek-tsee-yeh . . .
skiing	**skijanja** ski-yan-ya

*Men use the first alternative, women the second

I'd like lessons in . . .	**Želio/željela* bih lekcije . . .** shel-yo/shel-yel-ah beeh lek-tsee-yeh . . .
sailing	**jedrenja** yedren-ya
water skiing	**skijanja na moru** ski-yan-ya na moroo
sub-aqua diving	**ronjenja** ron-yen-ya
Can I hire . . .	**Htio/htjela* bih unajmiti . . .** h-tee-o/ht-yel-ah beeh oonaee-meetee . . .
a boat?	**čamac?** cham-ats
a fishing rod?	**trsku za ribarenje?** ter-skoo za reeba-renyeh
a deckchair?	**ležaljku?** lesh-alkoo
a sun umbrella?	**suncobran?** soon-tsobrun
the necessary equipment?	**potrebnu opremu?** pot-reb-noo oprem-oo
How much is it . . .	**Koliko košta . . .** kol-eeko koshta . . .
per day/per hour?	**na dan/na sat?** na dun/na sat
Do I need a licence?	**Treba li mi dozvola?** treb-a lee mee dozvol-ah

*Men use the first alternative, women the second

Asking if things are allowed

ESSENTIAL INFORMATION

- May one smoke here?
  May we smoke here?
  May I smoke here?
  Can one smoke here?
  Can we smoke here?
  Can I smoke here?

  Može li se pušiti ovdje?

- All these English variations can be expressed in one way in Serbo-Croat. To save space, only the first English version: May one . . .? is shown below.

WHAT TO SAY

Excuse me, please	**Izvinite molim**
	eez-*veen*-eet-eh m*o*l-im
May one . . .	**Može li se . . .**
	mosh-eh lee seh . . .
camp here?	**kampovati ovdje?**
	k*a*mpov-atee *o*vd-yeh
come in?	**ući?**
	*oo*chee
dance here?	**plesati ovdje?**
	ples-atee *o*vd-yeh
fish here?	**pecati ovdje?**
	ped-atee *o*v-d-yeh
get a drink here?	**dobiti piće ovdje?**
	d*o*b-eetee peecheh *o*vd-yeh
get out this way?	**izaći ovim putem**
	*ee*z-achee *o*v-im p*o*ot-em
get something to eat here?	**dobiti nešto za jesti ovdje?**
	d*o*b-etee nesh-to za yes-tee *o*v-dyeh
leave one's thing here?	**ostaviti svoje stvari ovdje?**
	*o*stav-eetee svoyeh stv*a*-ree *o*vd-yeh
look around?	**pogledati okolo?**
	p*o*gleh-da-tee *o*-kolo
park here?	**parkirati ovdje?**
	park*ee*r-atee *o*vd-veh

May one . . .	Može li se . . .
	mosh-eh lee seh . . .
sit here?	sjesti ovdje?
	s-yestee ovd-yeh
smoke here?	pušiti ovdje?
	poosh-eetee ovd-yeh
swim here?	plivati ovdje
	pleev-atee ovd-yeh
take photos here?	slikati ovdje?
	sleeka-tee ovd-yeh
telephone here?	telefonirati ovdje?
	telephon-eeratee ovd-yeh
wait here?	čekati ovdje?
	check-atee ovd-yeh

LIKELY REACTIONS

Yes, certainly	Da, sigurno
	da seeg-oornoh
Help yourself	Služite se
	sloosh-eeteh seh
I think so	Mislim da je tako
	mis-lim da yeh ta-ko
Of course	Sigurno
	seeg-oorno
Yes, but be careful	Da, ali pazite se
	da ah-lee paz-eeteh seh
No, certainly not	Ne, stvarno ne
	neh stvarno neh
I don't think so	Ne mislim da je tako
	neh mis-lim da yeh ta-ko
Not normally	Obično ne
	obeech-no neh
Sorry	Žao mi je
	sha-o mee yeh

Reference

PUBLIC NOTICES
- Key words on signs for drivers, pedestrians, travellers, shoppers and overnight guests.

AUTOPUT	Motorway
BAR	Bar
BESPLATAN ULAZ	Admission free
BIFE	Buffet
BOLNICA	Hospital
CARINARNICA	Customs
CESTARINA	Toll
ČEKAJ	Wait
ČEKAONICA	Waiting room
ČUVAJ SE PSA	Beware of the dog
DAME	Ladies
DOLAZAK	Arrivals
DOZVOLJENO PUŠITI	Smoking allowed
DRŽI SE NA DESNO	Keep right
DVOSMJERAN PROMET	Two way traffic
GARDEROBA	Left luggage
GOSPODA	Gentlemen
GURAJ	Push
HLADNO	Cold
IZDAJE SE SOBA	Room to rent
IZGUBLJENE STVARI	Lost property
IZLAZ	Exit
IZLAZ (AUTOPUTA)	Exit (from motorway)
IZLAZ ZA NUŽDU	Emergency exit
IZNAJMIVA SE	To rent
IZRAVAN PROMET	Through traffic
JEDAN SMJER	One way (street)
KASA (BLAGAJNA)	Cash desk
KAT (PRVI, DRUGI, TREĆI, PRIZEMLJE, PODRUM)	Floor (first, second, third, ground, basement)
KLIZOVITO	Slippery surface (road)
KRAJ (AUTOPUTA)	End (motorway)
KRAJ ZABRANE	End of parking restrictions
KUCAJ	Knock (door)
KUPAONICA	Bathroom
LAVINA	Avalanche area
LIFT	Lift

MEKANI RUBOVI	Soft shoulder
MILICIJA	Police
NA PRODAJU	For sale
NE DIRAJ	Do not touch
NEMA PRAZNO	No vacancies
NIJE PITKO	Not for drinking
NOSAČ (PORTIR)	Porter (hotels)
FAKIN	Porter (stations, ports)
ODLAZAK	Departures
ODRON KAMENA	Falling stones
OGRANIČENA BRZINA	Speed limit
OPASNO	Danger
OPASNA KRIVINA	Dangerous bend
OTVORENO	Open
OTVORENO OD . . . DO	Open from . . . to
PARKIRANJE	Car park
PARKIRANJE OGRANIČENO	Restricted parking
PAZI NA VLAK	Beware of the trains
PAZI/OPREZNO	Caution
PERON	Platform
PITKA VODA	Drinking water
PJEŠACI	Pedestrians
POČETAK AUTOPUTA	Start (motorway)
PODZEMAN PROLAZ	Subway
PODZEMNA ZELJEZNICA	Underground (train)
POMIČNE STEPENICE	Escalator
POPUST	Special offer
POTREBAN DISK ZA PARKIRANJE	Parking tokens required
POVRŠINA POKVARENA	Bad surface (road)
PRAZNO	Vacant
PREDNOST NA DESNO	Priority to the right
PREKO PRUGE	Level crossing
PREPUSTI	Yield
PRIJEĆI	Crossroads
PRIJELAZ ZA BICIKLE	Bike crossing
PRIVATNO	Private
PRODAJA KARATA	Ticket office
PROLAZ ZABRANJEN POD PRETNJOM GLOBE	Trespassers will be prosecuted
PROMETNA SVIJETLA (SEMAFOR)	Traffic lights
PROSTOR ZA STAJANJE	Standing room

PUT SE SUŽAVA	Road narrows
PUT ZA BICIKLE	Bike path
RADOVI NA PUTU	Construction
RASKRSNICA	Crossroads
RASPRODAJA	Sale
RECEPCIJA	Reception
REZERVACIJA	Reservations
REZERVIRANO	Reserved
SAMOPOSLUGA	Self-service
ŠKOLA	School
SKRETANJE	Detour
ŠKRIPAC	Dead end
STOJ	Halt/stop
SVIJETLA	Lights on
TOALETA	Toilet
TOPLO	Hot (tap)
TRPEZARIJA	Dining room
TUŠ	Shower
UDJI U TRAKU	Get in lane
ULAZ	Entrance
UPUTI	Guide
URED ZA INFORMACIJE	Information office
USPORAVAJ	Slow down
VAGON RESTORAN	Dining car
VELIKI NAGIB	Steep hill
VISOKI NAPON	High voltage
VLAK	Train
VOZI	Go
VOZI POLAGANO	Drive slowly
VUCI	Pull
ZA AUTOBUSE (SAMO)	For buses (only)
ZA TEŠKA KOLA	For heavy vehicles
ZA UNAJMITI	For hire
ZABRANJEN ULAZ	No admittance
ZABRANJENO	Forbidden
ZABRANJENO DIRATI	Do not touch
ZABRANJENO PARKIRANJE	No parking
ZABRANJENO PRETICANJE	Passing forbidden
ZABRANJENO PUŠITI	No smoking
ZABRANJENO SKRETANJE	No turning
ZATVORENO	Closed
ZATVORENO NEDJELJOM	Closed on Sundays
ZAUZETO	Engaged/occupied

ABBREVIATIONS

br	broj	number
Din	dinar	dinar
Dbk	Dubrovnik	Dubrovnik
gosp	gospodin	Mr
gdja	gospodja	Mrs
gdjica	gospodjica	Miss
god	godina	year
H	hladno	cold
h-s	hrvatsko-srpski	Croat-Serbian
itd	i tako dalje	etcetera
jedn	jednina	singular
mn	množina	plural
mr	muški rod	masculine gender
og	ove godine	this year
om	ovog mjeseca	this month
os	ove sedmice	this week
raz	razred	class
rkt	rimokatolik	Roman Catholic
SFRJ	Socijalistička Federativna Republika Jugoslavije	Socialist Federal Republic of Yugoslavia
SR	Socijalistička Republika	Socialist Republic
s-h	srpsko-hrvatski	Serbo-Croat
tel	telefon	telephone
tj	to jest	that is to say
ul	ulica	street
žr	ženski rod	feminine gender
adr	adresa	address
T	toplo	hot
trg	trgovina	trade
l	litar	litre
m	metar	metre
kg	kilogram	kilogram
pod	poduzeće	company
g	gram	gram
cm	centimetar	centimetre
km	kilometar	kilometre
kw	kilovat	kilowatt
£	funta	pound
SUP	Sekretaritjat Unutrašnjih Poslova	Home Office

JŽ	**Jugoslavenska Željeznica**	Yugoslav railways
AMSJ	**Automoto Savez Jugoslavije**	Yugoslavia Automobile Association
sv	**sveti**	saint

NUMBERS

Cardinal numbers

0	**nula**	noolah
1	**jedan**	yed-an
2	**dva**	dva
3	**tri**	tree
4	**četiri**	chet-eeree
5	**pet**	peht
6	**šest**	shehst
7	**sedam**	seh-dam
8	**'osam**	osam
9	**devet**	deh-vet
10	**deset**	deh-set
11	**jedanaest**	yeh-da-na-est
12	**dvanaest**	dvah-na-est
13	**trinaest**	tree-na-est
14	**četrnaest**	chet-er-na-est
15	**petnaest**	peht-na-est
16	**šesnaest**	shehst-na-est
17	**sedamnaest**	seh-dam-na-est
18	**osamnaest**	o-sam-na-est
19	**devetnaest**	deh-vet-na-est
20	**dvadeset**	dva-deh-set
21	**dvadeset jedan**	dva-deh-set yed-an'
22	**dvadeset dva**	dva-deh-set dva
23	**dvadeset tri**	dva-deh-set tree
24	**dvadeset četiri**	dva-deh-set chet-eeree
25	**dvadeset pet**	dva-deh-set peht
26	**dvadeset šest**	dva-deh-seh shehst
27	**dvadeset sedam**	dva-deh-set seh-dam
28	**dvadeset osam**	dva-deh-set o-sam
29	**dvadeset devet**	dva-deh-set deh-vet
30	**trideset**	tree-deh-set
31	**trideset jedan**	tree-deh-setyed-an
32	**trideset dva**	tree-des-set dva

40	četrdeset	chet-er-deh-set
41	četrdeset jedan	chet-er-deh-set yed-an
42	četrdeset dva	chet-er-deh-set dva
50	pedeset	peh-deh-set
51	pedeset jedan	peh-deh-set yed-an
52	pedeset dva	peh-deh-set dva
60	šezdeset	shehz-deh-set
61	šezdeset jedan	shehz-deh-set yed-an
62	šezdeset dva	shehz-deh-set dva
70	sedamdeset	seh-dam-deh-set
71	sedamdeset jedan	seh-dam-deh-set yed-an
72	sedamdeset dva	seh-dam-deh-set dva
80	osamdeset	o-sam-deh-set
81	osamdeset jedan	o-sam-deh-set yed-an
82	osamdeset dva	o-sam-deh-set dva
90	devedeset	deh-vet-deh-set
91	devedeset jedan	deh-vet-deh-set yed-an
92	devedeset dva	deh-vet-deh-set dva
100	sto	sto
101	sto jedan	sto yed-an
110	sto deset	sto deh-set
120	sto dvadeset	sto dva-deh-set
200	dvjesta	dvee-yeh-sta
300	trista	tree-sta
400	cetrsto	chet-er-sto
500	petsto	peht-sto
600	sesto	sheh-sto
700	sedamsto	seh-dam-sto
800	osamsto	o-sam-sto
900	devetsto	deh-vet-sto
1,000	hiljada/tisuća	heel-ya-da/tees-oocha
2,000	dvije hiljade	dvee-yeh heel-ya-deh
3,000	tri hiljade	tree heel-ya-deh
10,000	deset hiljada	deh-set heel-yada
100,000	sto hiljada	sto heel-ya-da
1,000,000	milijun	meelee-yoon

Ordinal numbers

1st	**prvi**	per-vee
2nd	**drugi**	droo-ghee
3rd	**treći**	trechee
4th	**četvrti**	chet-ver-tee
5th	**peti**	peh-tee
6th	**šesti**	shes-tee
7th	**sedmi**	sed-mee
8th	**osmi**	os-mee
9th	**deveti**	deh-veh-tee
10th	**deseti**	deh-seh-tee
11th	**jedanaesti**	yed-ana-estee
12th	**dvanaesti**	dva-na-estee

TIME

What time is it?	**Koliko je sati?**
	kol-eeko yeh sa-tee
It's . . . (this is not translated in Serbo-Croat)	
one o'clock	**jedan sat**
	yed-an sat
two o'clock	**dva sata**
	dva sa-ta
three o'clock	**tri sata**
	tree sa-ta
four o'clock	**četiri sata**
	chet-eeree sa-ta
in the morning	**u jutro**
	oo yoo-tro
in the afternoon	**poslije podne**
	poslee-veh pod-neh
in the evening	**u veče**
	oo veh-cheh
at night	**noću**
	no-choo
It's . . . (this is not translated in Serbo-Croat)	
noon	**podne**
	pod-neh
midnight	**ponoć**
	po-noch
It's . . . (this is not translated in Serbo-Croat)	
five past five	**pet i pet**
	peht ee peht
ten past five	**pet i deset**
	peht ee deh-set
a quarter past five	**pet i petnaest**
	peht ee peht-na-est
twenty past five	**pet i dvadeset**
	peht ee dva-deh set
twenty-five past five	**pet i dvadeset pet**
	peht ee dva-deh-set peht
half past five	**pola šest**
	po-la shehst
twenty-five to six	**dvadeset pet do šest**
	dva-deh-set peht doh shehst
twenty to six	**dvadeset do šest**
	dva-deh-set doh shehst

a quarter to six	**petnaest do šest**
	peht-na-est doh shehst
ten to six	**deset do šest**
	deh-set doh shehst
five to six	**pet do šest**
	peht doh shehst
At what time . . . (does the train leave)?	**U koliko sato . . . (odlazi voz za)?**
	oo kol-eeko sa-tee . . . (odlaz-ee voz za)
At . . .	**U . . .**
	oo . . .
13.00	**trinaest (sati)**
	tree-na-est (sa-tee)
14.05	**četrnaest i pet**
	chet-er-na-est ee peht
15.10	**petnaest i deset**
	peht-na-est ee deh-set
16.15	**šesnaest i petnaest**
	shehst-na-est ee peht-na-est
17.20	**sedamnaest i dvadeset**
	seh-dam-na-est ee dva-deh-set
18.25	**osamnaest i dvadeset pet**
	o-sam-na-est ee dva-deh-set peht
19.30	**devetnaest i trideset**
	deh-vet-na-est ee tree-deh-set
20.35	**dvadeset i trideset pet**
	dva-deh-set ee tree-deh-set peht
21.40	**dvadeset jedan i četrdeset**
	dva-deh-set yed-an ee chet-er-deh-set
22.45	**dvadeset dva i cetrdeset pet**
	dva-deh-set dvah ee chet-er-deh-set peht
23.50	**dvadeset tri i pedeset**
	dva-deh-set tree ee peht-deh-set
0.55	**nula pedeset pet**
	noola peht-deh-set peht
in ten minutes	**za deset minuta**
	za deh-set meen-oota
in a quarter of an hour	**za petnaest minuta**
	za peht-na-est meen-oota
in half an hour	**za pola sata**
	za po-la sa-ta
in three quarters of an hour	**za četrdeset pet minuta**
	za chet-er-deh-set peht meen-oota

DAYS

Monday	**ponedjeljak** poned-yel-yak
Tuesday	**utorak** ooto-rak
Wednesday	**srijeda** sree-yeda
Thursday	**četvrtak** chet-ver-tak
Friday	**petak** peh-tak
Saturday	**subota** soo-bota
Sunday	**nedjelja** ned-yel-ya
last Monday	**prošli ponedjeljak** prosh-lee poned-yel-yak
next Tuesday	**sljedeći utorak** sleeyeh-deh-chee ootorak
on Wednesday	**u srijedu** oo sree-yedoo
on Thursday	**u četvrtak** oo chet-ver-tak
until Friday	**do petka** doh peht-ka
before Saturday	**prije subote** pree-yeh sooboteh
after Sunday	**poslije nedjelje** pos-lee-yeh ned-yel-yeh
the day before yesterday	**prekjučer** prek-yoo-cher
two days ago	**pred dva dana** pred dva da-na
yesterday	**jučer** yoo-cher
yesterday morning	**jučer u jutro** yoo-cher oo yoo-tro
yesterday afternoon	**jučer poslije podne** yoo-cher pos-lee-yeh pod-ne
last night	**sinoč** see-noch

today	**danas**
	dan-us
this morning	**jutros**
	yoot-ros
this afternoon	**danas poslije podne**
	dan-us pos-lee-yeh pod-neh
tonight	**večeras**
	vech-airas
tomorrow	**sutra**
	sootra
tomorrow morning	**sutra u jutro**
	sootra oo yoo-tro
tomorrow afternoon	**sutra poslije podne**
	sootra pos-lee-yeh pod-neh
tomorrow evening	**sutra u veče**
	sootra oo vecheh
tomorrow night	**sutra noću**
	sootra nochoo
the day after tomorrow	**prekosutra**
	preko-sootra

MONTHS AND DATES

January	**januar**
	ya-noo-ar
February	**februar**
	feh-broo-ar
March	**mart**
	mart
April	**april**
	ap-reel
May	**maj**
	ma-ee
June	**juni**
	yoo-nee
July	**juli**
	yoo-lee
August	**august**
	ah-oo-goost
September	**septembar**
	sep-tem-bar

October	**oktobar**
	okto-bar
November	**novembar**
	novem-bar
December	**decembar**
	deh-tsem-bar
in January	**u januaru**
	oo ya-noo-ah-roo
until February	**do februara**
	doh feh-broo-ah-ra
before March	**prije marta**
	pree-yeh mar-ta
after April	**poslije aprila**
	pos-lee-yeh ap-reela'
during May	**kroz maj**
	kroz ma-ee
not until June	**ne do juna**
	neh doh yoo-na
the beginning of July	**početkom jula**
	pocket-kom yoo-la
the middle of August	**polovinom augusta**
	polo-veen-om ah-oo-goos-ta
the end of September	**svršetkom septembra**
	sver-shet-kom sep-tem-bra
last month	**prošli mjesec**
	prosh-lee m-yes-ets
this month	**ovaj mjesec**
	ov-aee m-yes-ets
next month	**slijedeči mjesec**
	slee-yed-echee m-yes-ets
in spring	**u prolječe**
	oo prol-yeh-cheh
in summer	**ljeti**
	l-yeh-tee
in autumn	**u jesen**
	oo yeh-sen
in winter	**zimi**
	zeemee
this year	**ove godine**
	ov-eh god-eeneh
last year	**prošle godine**
	prosh-leh god-eeneh

next year	**slijedeče godine**
	slee-*yed*-echeh g*o*d-eeneh
in 1982	**hiljadu devet sto osamdeset druge godine**
	h*ee*l-ya-doo deh-vet sto *o*sam-deh-set dr*oo*gheh g*o*d-eeneh
in 1985	**hiljadu devet sto osamdeset pete godine**
	h*ee*l-ya-doo deh-vet sto *o*sam-deh-set p*e*h-teh g*o*d-eeneh
in 1990	**hiljadu devet sto devedesete godine**
	h*ee*l-ya-doo deh-vet sto deh-vet-deh-set-eh g*o*d-eeneh
What's the date today?	**Koji je datum danas?**
	k*o*yee yeh d*a*-toom d*a*n-us
It's the 6th of March	**Šesti mart**
	sh*e*h-stee m*a*rt
It's the 12th of April	**Dvanaesti april**
	dv*a*-na-estee *a*p-reel
It's the 21st of August	**Dvadeset prvi august**
	dv*a*deh-set '*er*-vee *o*w-goost

Public holidays

Offices, shops and schools are all closed on the following dates.

1–2 January	**Nova godina**	New Year holiday
1–2 May	**Prvi Maj**	Labour Day
4 July	**Dan borca**	Fighter's Day
29–30 November	**Dan Republike**	Days of the Republic

Republican national holidays

Serbia 7 July
Montenegro 13 July
Slovenia 22 July
Croatia, Bosnia and Herzegovina 27 July
Macedonia 2 August and 11 October

COUNTRIES AND NATIONALITIES

Countries

Albania	**Albanija** *a*lba-nee-ya
Australia	**Australija** *ah*-oo-stral-ya
Austria	**Austrija** *ah*-oo-stri-ya
Belgium	**Belgija** b*e*l-ghee-ya
Britain	**Britanija** br*e*etan-eeya
Canada	**Kanada** k*a*-nah-da
Croatia	**Hrvatska** her-v*a*t-ska
East Africa	**Istočna Afrika** *ee*stoch-na *a*frika
Eire	**Irska** *ee*r-ska
England	**Engleska** *e*n-gleska
France	**Francuska** fr*a*n-tsoo-ska
Germany	**Nijemačka** nee-y*e*h-mach-ka
Greece	**Grčka** g*e*rch-ka
Hungary	**Madjarska** m*a*h-jar-ska
India	**Indija** *i*ndee-ya
Italy	**Italija** *i*talee-ya
Luxembourg	**Luksemburg** l*oo*x-em-boorg
Netherlands	**Nizozemska** n*ee*zo-zemska
New Zealand	**Novi Zeland** n*o*vee z*e*hland
Northern Ireland	**Sjeverna Irska** s-y*e*v-airna *ee*r-ska

Pakistan	**Pakistan**
	pak-eestan
Portugal	**Portugal**
	port-oogal
Romania	**Rumunija**
	roo-moo-nee-ya
Russia	**Rusija**
	roosee-ya
Scotland	**Škotska**
	sh-kot-ska
South Africa	**Južna Afrika**
	yoosh-na afrika
Spain	**Španija**
	shpanee-ya
Switzerland	**Švicarska**
	shvi-tsar-ska
United States	**Amerika**
	amerika
Wales	**Vels**
	vehls
West Indies	**Karibi**
	karee-bee
Yugoslavia	**Jugoslavija**
	yoogoslav-eeya

Nationalities
[*Use the first alternative for men, the second for women*]

Albanian	**Albanac/Albanka**
	alb*a*-nats/*a*lban-ka
American	**Amerikanac/Amerikanka**
	amerik-*a*n-a*ts/ameri*kanka
Australian	**Australac/Au̯straljka**
	ah-oo-stral-ats/*ah*-oo-stral-ka
Canadian	**Kanadjanin/Kanadjanka**
	kan*a*j-aneen/k*a*naj-anka
East African	**Istočni Afrikanac/Istočna afrikanka**
	*ee*st-och-nee afrik*a*n-ats/*ee*stoch-na
	afri*k*anka
English	**Englez/Engleskinja**
	*e*n-glez/englez-skeen-ya
German	**Nijemac/Nijemica**
	nee-yeh-mats/nee-yeh-meetsa
Hungarian	**Madjar/Madjarica**
	m*a*h-jar/m*a*h-jar-eetsa
Indian	**Indus/Induskinja**
	*i*ndoos/indoos-keen-ya
Irish	**Irac/Irkinja**
	*ee*rats/*ee*rkeen-ya
New Zealander	**Novo Zelandez/Novo Zeladjanka**
	n*o*vo zel-andez/n*o*vo zelaj-anka
Pakistani	**Pakistanac/Pakistanka**
	pakeest*a*n-ats/pakeest*a*nka
Romanian	**Rumun/Rumunjka**
	r*oo*-moon/r*oo*-moon-ka
Russian	**Rus/Ruskinja**
	r*oo*s/r*oo*s-keen-ya
Scots	**Škot/Škotkinja**
	shk*o*t/shk*o*t-keen-ya
South African	**Južni Afrikanac/Južna Afrikanka**
	y*oo*sh-nee afrik*a*n-ats/y*oo*sh-na
	afrikanka
Welsh	**Velšanin/Velšanka**
	v*e*lsh-anin/v*e*lshanka
West Indian	**Iz Kariba**
	eez kar*ee*-ba
Yugoslav	**Jugoslaven/Jugoslavenka**
	yoogosl*a*ven/yoogoslav-enka

DEPARTMENT STORE GUIDE

Alati	Tools
Auto oprema	Car accessories
Blagajna	Cash
Bluze	Blouses
Brodska oprema	Boat accessories
Čarape	Stockings
Četvrti	Fourth
Ćilimi	Carpets
Darovi	Gifts
Dječje igračke	Toys
Dragulji	Jewellery
Drugi	Second (floor)
Donje rublje	Underclothes
Donje rublje za dame	Underwear (women)
Električni aparati	Electrical appliances
Fotografia	Photography
Frizerski salon	Hairdresser
Gramofonske ploče	Records
Grudnjaci	Bras
Gvoždje	Laminates
Hrana	Food
Informacije	Information
Jastuci	Cushions
Kamping	Camping
Kamp oprema	Camping requisites
Keramika	Ceramics
Knjige	Books
Konfekcijska odjeća	Ready-made clothing
Kozmetika	Cosmetics
Kožna galanterija	Leather goods
Kravate	Ties
Kristal	Crystal
Krojački pribor	Haberdashery
Kućni namještaj	Home furnishings
Kuhinjski namještaj	Kitchen furniture
Moda za dame	Ladies fashion
Obuća	Shoes
Odio košulja	Shirt department
Oprema za novorodjenče	Layette
Papirnica	Stationery
Parfumerija	Perfumery
Pisaće potrebštine	Stationery

Podrum	Basement
Pojasi	Belts
Pokrivači	Blankets
Pokućstvo	Furniture
Porculan	China
Posteljina	Bedding
Posudje	Crockery
Prizemlje	Ground (floor)
Prvi	First (floor)
Puloveri	Pullovers
Pušenje zabranjeno	No smoking
Radio aparati	Radios
Ribo-materijal	Fishing gear
Rublje	Linen
Sanitarije	Bathroom requisites
Satovi	Watches – clocks
Suveniri	Souvenirs
Kat	Floor
Sredstva za čišćenje	Cleaning materials
Staklarija	Glassware
Steznici	Girdles
Sve za putovanje	Travel articles
Šeširi	Millinery
Štofovi	Materials/fabrics
Televizija	Television
Tekstil za kuću	Furnishing fabrics
Treći	Third (floor)
'Uradi-sam' (za hobiste)	Do-it-yourself
Za damu/za dame	Ladieswear
Za djecu	Child
Za muškarce	Menswear
Zastori/zavjesi	Curtains
Zemljano sudje	Earthenware
Željeznarija	Hardware

CONVERSION TABLES

Read the centre column of these tables from right to left to convert
from metric to imperial and from left to right to convert from
imperial to metric e.g. 5 litres = 8.80 pints; 5 pints = 2.84 litres

pints		litres
1.76	1	0.57
3.52	2	1.14
5.28	3	1.70
7.07	4	2.27
8.80	5	2.84
10.56	6	3.41
12.32	7	3.98
14.08	8	4.55
15.84	9	5.11

gallons		litres
0.22	1	4.55
0.44	2	9.09
0.66	3	13.64
0.88	4	18.18
1.00	5	22.73
1.32	6	27.28
1.54	7	31.82
1.76	8	36.37
1.98	9	40.91

ounces		grams
0.04	1	28.35
0.07	2	56.70
.0.11	3	85.05
0.14	4	113.40
0.18	5	141.75
0.21	6	170.10
0.25	7	198.45
0.28	8	226.80
0.32	9	255.15

pounds		kilos
2.20	1	0.45
4.41	2	0.91
6.61	3	1.36
8.82	4	1.81
11.02	5	2.27
13.23	6	2.72
15.43	7	3.18
17.64	8	3.63
19.84	9	4.08

inches		centimetres
0.39	1	2.54
0.79	2	5.08
1.18	3	7.62
1.58	4	10.16
1.95	5	12.70
2.36	6	15.24
2.76	7	17.78
3.15	8	20.32
3.54	9	22.86

yards		metres
1.09	1	0.91
2.19	2	1.83
3.28	3	2.74
4.37	4	3.66
5.47	5	4.57
6.56	6	5.49
7.66	7	6.40
8.65	8	7.32
9.84	9	8.23

miles		kilometres
0.62	1	1.61
1.24	2	3.22
1.86	3	4.83
2.49	4	6.44
3.11	5	8.05
3.73	6	9.66
4.35	7	11.27
4.97	8	12.87
5.59	9	14.48

A quick way to convert kilometres to miles: divide by 8 and multiply by 5. To convert miles to kilometres: divide by 5 and multiply by 8.

fahrenheit (°F)	centigrade (°C)		lbs/ sq in	k/ sq cm
212°	100°	boiling point	18	1.3
100°	38°		20	1.4
98.4°	36.9°	body temperature	22	1.5
86°	30°		25	1.7
77°	25°		29	2.0
68°	20°		32	2.3
59°	15°		35	2.5
50°	10°		36	2.5
41°	5°		39	2.7
32°	0°	freezing point	40	2.8
14°	−10°		43	3.0
−4°	−20°		45	3.2
			46	3.2
			50	3.5
			60	4.2

To convert °C to °F, divide by 5, multiply by 9 and add 32. To convert °F to °C, take away 32, divide by 9 and multiply by 5.

CLOTHING SIZES

Remember – always try on clothes before buying.
Clothing sizes are usually unreliable.

women's dresses and suits

Europe	38	40	42	44	46	48
UK	32	34	36	38	40	42
USA	10	12	14	16	18	20

men's suits and coats

Europe	46	48	50	52	54	56
UK and USA	36	38	40	42	44	46

men's shirts

Europe	36	37	38	39	41	42	43
UK and USA	14	14½	15	15½	16	16½	17

socks

Europe	38–39	39–40	40–41	41–42	42–43
UK and USA	9½	10	10½	11	11½

shoes

Europe	34	35½	36½	38	39	41	42	43	44	45
UK	2	3	4	5	6	7	8	9	10	11
USA	3½	4½	5½	6½	7½	8½	9½	10½	11½	12½

Do it yourself

Some notes on the language

This section does not deal with 'Grammar' as such. The purpose here is to explain some of the most obvious and elementary nuts and bolts of the language, based on the principal phrases included in the book. This information should enable you to produce numerous sentences of your own making.

There is no pronunciation guide in most of this section, partly because it would get in the way of the explanations and partly because you have to do it yourself at this stage if you are serious – work out the pronunciation from all the earlier examples in the book.

NOUNS

All nouns in Serbo-Croat belong to one of three genders: masculine, feminine or neuter, irrespective of whether they refer to living things or inanimate object.

As in many other languages, Serbo-Croat nouns have different forms according to their *gender* (masculine, feminine or neuter) and to their *number* (singular or plural). However, unlike some well-known European languages (French, Spanish, Italian) they also change according to their function in the sentence (subject, object, etc.) i.e. according to their *case*. There are seven cases in Serbo Croat.

Does getting these different forms correct matter? Not unless you want to make a serious attempt to speak correctly and scratch beneath the surface of the language. You would probably be understood if you use the wrong form providing your pronunciation was good.

In order to practise the basic phrases used in this section only *two* cases will be introduced.

Singular nouns

	masculine	feminine	neuter
the/an address		adresa	
the/an apple		jabuka	
the/a bill	račun		
the/a bottle of wine		boca vina	
the/a chicken			pile
the/a cup of tea		šalica čaja	
the/an egg			jaje
the/a glass of beer	čaša piva		
the/a key	ključ		
the/a menu	jelovnik		
the/a receipt		priznanica	
the/a room		soba	
the/a sandwich	sendvič		
the/a suitcase	kofer		
the/a timetable	red		

Important things to remember

- You can often tell if a noun is masculine, feminine or neuter by its ending. When they are the subject of a sentence (Nominative Case), masculine nouns in the singular usually end in a consonant, feminine nouns in -a and neuter nouns in -e or -o. Look at the examples in the table above.

- No word is used normally for *the, a, some* or *any* in Serbo Croat. If we take as an English example *Where is the suitcase?*, the Serbo-Croat translation **Gdje je kofer?** would mean literally *Where is suitcase?* Similarly, *Have you got any coffee?* would translate as **Imate li kavu?**, literally *Have you got coffee?* You can guess whether you would say *a* or *the* etc. in English from the context of the sentence. However, if you wish to specify the quantity *I'll have a (one) doughnut* you can use **jedan** (*one*): **Htio/htjela bih jedan krafen.**

- ! Caution

  In phrases beginning: I'll have . . .

  Have you got . . .?

  I'd like . . .

  Where can I get . . .?

Serbo-Croat nouns become the object of the sentence (called the Accusative Case) and the endings of the *feminine* singular nouns change from -a to -u, e.g. **adresa** becomes **adresu.**

Practice saying and writing these sentences in Serbo-Croat. Watch for the caution sign (!) and note that *I'd like/I'll have* change their construction according to whether you are a man (**želio/htio**) or a woman (**željela/htjela**). You will have seen examples of this throughout the phrase book.

Where is the key?	**Gdje je ključ**
Where is the suitcase?	**Gdje je . . .?**
Where is the address?	**. . .**
Have you got the timetable?	**Imate li red?**
!Have you got the address?	**Imate li . . .?**
Have you got the menu?	**. . .**
!I'd like a glass of beer	**Želio/željela bih čašu piva**

(Note that **piva** 'of beer' and later **čaja** 'of tea' and **vina** 'of wine' do not change their endings.)

I'd like the bill	**Želio/željela bih . . .**
!I'd like an apple	**. . .**
!I'd like the receipt	**. . .**
!Where can I get a cup of tea?	**Gdje mogu dobiti šalicu čaja?**
Where can I get the key?	**Gdje mogu dobiti . . . ?**
!Where can I get a room?	**. . .**
!I'll have a bottle of wine	**Htio/htjela bih bocu vina**
!I'll have a glass of beer	**Htio/htjela bih . . .**
I'll have the chicken	**. . .**

Now make up more sentences along the same lines. Try adding please: **molim** at the beginning or the end.

Note that if you just want to ask for:

A glass of beer, please   **Čašu piva, molim**
the noun 'a glass' must be in the Accusative Case because the phrase *I'd like* or *I'll have* is understood although not said.

Now practise plural nouns on the next page.

Plural nouns

Look at the table below; note that some of the examples don't follow the basic rule (see 'Important things to remember' below) and need to be memorized.

	masculine	feminine	neuter
addresses		**adrese**	
apples		**jabuke**	
bills	**računi**		
bottles of wine		**boce vina**	
chickens			**pilići**
cups of tea		**šalice čaja**	
eggs			**jaja**
glasses of beer		**čaše piva**	
keys	**ključevi**		
menus	**jelovnici**		
receipts		**priznanice**	
rooms		**sobe**	
sandwiches	**sendviči**		
suitcases	**koferi**		
timetables	**redovi**		

Important things to remember

- When they are the subject of the sentence (Nominative Case), most masculine nouns in the plural end in **-i**.
- Some masculine nouns of one syllable form the plural by adding **-evi** or **-ovi**, e.g. **ključ** becomes **ključevi** and **red** becomes **redovi**.
- Most feminine nouns end in **-e**.
- Most neuter nouns end in **-a**.
- ! Caution
  In phrases beginning:
  I'll have . . .
  Have you got . . . ?
  I'd like . . .
  Where can I get . . .?
  as in the singular, Serbo-Croat nouns become the object of the sentence (Accusative Case) but in the plural, the endings of *masculine* nouns change from **-i** to **-e**, e.g. **računi** becomes **račune**.

- If a number is used with a plural noun e.g. *two* chickens, *five* children, the endings of the noun change according to *which* number! You will see examples of this throughout the book.

Practice saying and writing these sentences in Serbo-Croat. Watch for the caution sign (!) and remember that the words for *of wine/of beer/of tea* (**vina/piva/čaja**) always remains the same:

Where are the eggs?	**Gdje su jaja?**
Where are the suitcases?	**Gdje su . . .?**
Where are the bottles of wine?	**. . .**
!Have you got any sandwiches?	**Imate li sendviče**
Have you got any rooms?	**Imate li . . .?**
!Have you got the keys?	**. . .**
I'd like some apples	**Želio/željela bih . . .**
I'd like some eggs	**. . .**
Where can I get some bottles of wine?	**Gdje mogu dobiti . . .?**
!Where can I get the keys?	**. . .**
!Where can I get some suitcases?	**. . .**
!I'll have the sandwiches	**Htio/htjela bih . . .**
I'll have the bottles of wine	**. . .**

THIS AND THAT

Use these two words in Serbo-Croat
ovo (this)
to (that)
If you don't know the Serbo-Croat name for an object, just point and say:

Htio/htjela bih ovo	I'll have this
Želio/željela bih to	I'd like that

Now study the verbs on the next page.

HELPING OTHERS

You can help yourself with such phrases as:

I'd like . . . the bill	Želio/željela bih . . . račun
Where can I get . . . a cup of tea?	Gdje mogu dobiti . . . šalicu čaja?
I'll have . . . a glass of beer	Htio/htjela bih . . . čašu piva

If you come across a compatriot having trouble making himself **or** herself understood, you should be able to speak to the Yugoslav person on their behalf. Note that *he, she, we* and *they* are not usually translated in Serbo-Croat. (A pronunciation guide is provided from here on.)

He'd like . . .	**Želio bi račun**
	sh*e*l-yoo bee r*a*ch-oon
She'd like . . .	**Željela bi račun**
	sh*e*l-yel-a bee r*a*ch-oon
Where can he get . . .?	**Gdje može dobiti šalicu čaja?**
	gd-y*e*h m*o*sh-eh d*o*b-eetee shal-eetsoo cha-ya
Where can she get . . .?	**Gdje može dobiti šalicu čaja?**
	gd-y*e*h m*o*sh-eh d*o*b-eetee shal-eetsoo cha-ya
He'll have . . .	**Htio bi čašu piva**
	ht*ee*-o bee ch*a*sh-oo p*ee*va
She'll have . . .	**Htjela bi čašu piva**
	ht-yelah bee ch*a*sh-oo p*ee*va

You can also help a couple or a group if *they* are having difficulties:

They'd like . . .	**Željeli bi račun**
	sh*e*l-yel-ee bee r*a*ch-roon
Where can they get . . .?	**Gdje mogu dobiti šalicu čaja?**
	gd-y*e*h m*o*g-oo d*o*b-eetee shal-eetsoo cha-ya
They'll have . . .	**Htjeli bi čašu piva**
	hty-elee bee ch*a*sh-oo p*ee*va

What about the two of you? Just watch for the verb ending:

We'd like . . .	**Željeli bi račun**
	shel-jel-ee bee ra*ch*-oon
Where can we get . . .?	**Gdje možemo dobiti šalicu čaja?**
	gd-yeh mosh-eh-mo dob-eetee
	sh*a*l-eetsoo
We'll have . . .	**Htjeli bi čašu piva**
	ht-yelee bee ch*a*sh-oo p*ee*va

Try writing out your own checklist for these useful phrase starters, like this (notice the similarities):

I'd like . . .	**Želio bih . . ./Željela bih . . .**
He'd like . . .	**Želio bi . . .**
She'd like . . .	**Željela bi . . .**
We'd like . . .	**Željeli bi . . .**
They'd like . . .	**Željeli bi . . .**
Where can I get . . .?	**Gdje mogu dobiti . . .?**
Where can he get . . .?	**Gdje može dobiti . . .?**
Where can she get . . .?	**. . .**
Where can we get . . .?	**. . . .**
Where can they get . . .?	**. . .**
I'll have . . .	**Htio bih . . ./Htjela bih . . .**
He'll have . . .	**. . .**
She'll have . . .?	**. . .**
We'll have . . .?	**. . .**
They'll have . . .?	**. .**

MORE PRACTICE

On p. 150 are some more Serbo-Croat names of things. See how many different sentences you can make up, using the various points of information given earlier in this section. These nouns are all in the Nominative Case, as they would be in a dictionary but the change of ending needed in the Accusative Case is also noted.

		singular	plural
1	ashtray	**pepeljara** (*f*) **-u**	**pepeljare**
2	bag	**torba** (*f*) **-u**	**torbe**
3	bank	**banka** (*f*) **-u**	**banke**
4	biscuit	**keks** (*m*)	**keksi, -e**
5	car	**auto** (*m*)	**automobili, -e**
6	cigarette	**cigareta** (*f*) **-u**	**cigarete**
7	garage	**garaža** (*f*) **-u**	**garaže**
8	grape	**grozd** (*m*)	**grožđje**
9	guide book	**vodič** (*m*)	**vodiči, -e**
10	ice-cream	**sladoled** (*m*)	**sladoledi, -e**
11	melon	**dinja** (*f*) **-u**	**dinje**
12	passport	**pasoš** (*m*)	**pososi, -e**
13	plate	**tanjur** (*m*)	**tanjuri, -e**
14	postcard	**dopisnica** (*f*), **-u**	**dopisnice**
15	salad	**salata** (*f*) **-u**	**salate**
16	shoe	**cipela** (*f*) **-u**	**cipele**
17	stamp	**marka** (*f*) **-u**	**marke**
18	station	**stanica** (*f*) **-u**	**stanice**
19	sunglasses		**naočali za sunce** (*m*) **-e**
20	suntan oil	**ulje za sunčanje** (*n*)	**ulja za sunčanje**
21	sweet	**slatkiš** (*m*)	**slatkiši, -e**
22	telephone	**telefon** (*m*)	**telefoni, -e**
23	ticket	**karta** (f) **-u**	**karte**

Index

abbreviations 124–5
accommodation, *see* camping;
   hotel; renting accommodation;
   youth hostel
address 18, 41, 99
airport 20, 113
art gallery 20, 116

baker 21, 61–2
bank 21, 104, 150
banker's card 104, 105
bar 35, 80–82, 83, 121
battery (car) 107, 109
beach 20, 113
bills, paying 31, 82, 87, 110,
   120
books 46, 117
border crossing 14–15, 97
bread 66
   baker's 61–2
   restaurant 87
breakdown (car) 106, 107, 110
breakfast 28, 30, 32
bus 20, 25, 115
   destinations 113, 114
   information 112
   stop 21, 112, 113, 114
   times 26, 113
business 16, 19
butcher 21, 69, 75–6

cabaret 117
café 21, 80–84
cakes 21, 62–3
camping 21, 26, 33–7
   equipment 36
car 21, 34, 150
   breakdown 106, 107, 110
   documents 14, 98, 110, 111
   hire 110–11
   parts 110–11
   petrol 22, 106, 107

caravan 33, 34
change bureau 21, 104
chemist 21, 42–5, 92
cheques 104, 105
church 21
cigarettes 16, 48–9, 150
cinema 21, 116
clothing 50–53
   material 53
   measurements 50, 52
   sizes 52, 141
coins and notes 56–7, 102, 103,
   104–5, 124
cold meats 70, 71, 83
colours 53
compass points 18
complaints 97–8
concert 116, 117
conversion tables 139–40
concert hall 21
cooking terms 75, 88–91
countries 18, 100–101, 102,
   105, 134–5
courses at meals 87–8
craft shops 46
credit cards 59
currencies 104–5
customs 14–15, 121
cuts of meat 75–6

dairy bars 85
dancing 22, 116
dates 131–3
days of the week 41, 111, 130–
   131
delicatessen 21, 69
dentist 22, 92, 93, 94, 96
department store 22, 46
   guide 137–8
desserts 88
directions 20, 21, 24–5, 97
disco 22, 116

doctor 22, 92, 96
documents 14, 28, 32, 37, 99
  car 14, 98, 110, 111
drinks 16, 68, 80–82, 144, 145,
  146, 147, 148
dry-cleaning 22, 31

electrical equipment 36, 37, 38,
  39, 40, 54, 55
emergencies 39–41, 97
entertainment 116–18
expressions, everyday 12–13
eyes 42, 92, 93–4

family 17–18
film (camera) 46, 47
film (cinema) 117
first aid 43–4, 92
fish 22, 67, 70, 71, 77–9
food, shopping for 61–79
forms, official 15
friends 17
fruit 67, 72–4, 144–7, 150

garage 22, 106, 150
garden, public 21, 23, 116
gas 38, 39, 40, 54
grammar 143
greengrocer 22
  see also vegetables
greetings 12, 16, 58
grocer 22, 69
guide book 46, 117, 150

hairdresser 22
hardware 22, 54, 58
health care 92–6
hire, car 110–11
hire, sports equipment 118
holidays, public 133
hospital 22, 96, 121
hotel facilities and services 22,
  26, 28–32
household articles 38–40, 54–5
household cleaning
  materials 54, 55

ice-creams 22, 64, 150
illness 42, 92–6
information service
  (tourist) 21, 26–7, 112, 123
insurance 14, 92, 110
introductions 17

kitchen equipment 35, 38–40,
  54–5

language difficulties 143–50
laundry 22, 31, 35
leisure 116–18
lessons 117–18
letters 100–101
licence, driving 14, 98, 111
loss (of possessions) 98

map 11, 20, 46
markets 72, 77, 113, 114
materials (clothes) 53
measurements, body 50, 52
measurements, metric 24, 139–
  140
meat 67, 75–6, 87, 90–91
  cold 70, 71, 83
medical treatment 92, 95–6
medicines 42, 95
meeting people 16–19
menus 85, 86, 87, 88–91, 144,
  145, 146
money 14, 31, 32, 59, 99, 103,
  104–5
months of the year 131–3
motoring, *see* car
museum 22, 116

names 16, 41
nationalities 15, 18, 136
newspaper 22, 46
nightclub 22, 116
notes and coins 56–7, 102, 103, 104–5, 124
notices, public 121–3
nouns 143–4, 145, 146–7
numbers 24, 29, 32, 37, 56, 102, 103, 106, 125–7

official forms 15
oil (car) 106, 107

pain 92–5
parcels 101
park 22
parts of the body 92–3
passport 14, 15, 28, 33, 97, 99, 100, 104, 105, 150
permission, asking 58–9, 76, 97–8, 119–20, 145, 147
personal effects 44–5, 98–9
personal hygiene 44–5
petrol 22, 106, 107
photography 46, 47
picnic food 69–71
place names 20–23
plumbing 38, 39, 40
police 14, 20, 97, 122
politeness 12, 20–21, 58, 121, 122, 145, 147
poor quality goods 97–8
port authority 97
post box 23, 100, 102
post office 20, 100–101
postcards 46, 100, 101, 150
poste restante 100
problems
  camping 36–7
  car 107, 110
  complaints 97–8

electrical 39
gas 39, 40
health 92–6
loss 98
plumbing 38, 39, 40
theft 98–9
programme 117
pronunciation system 8–9
public
  buildings 20, 21, 116
  gardens 21, 23, 116
  holidays 133
  notices 121–3
  transport 25, 112–15

radiator (car) 107, 109
railway, see station (railway); train
reference section 121–41
relaxing 116–18
renting accommodation 38–41
restaurant 23, 26, 35, 85–91
road signs 106, 121–3
rubbish (refuse) 35, 41

salads 69, 70, 150
sandwiches 83–4, 144, 146, 147
savoury food 70–71, 83–4, 89–91
seasons 132
shellfish 77–8, 79, 89, 91
shoes 50, 52, 141, 150
shopping 35, 42–55, 137–8
  for food 61–79
  language 56, 58–60
  names of departments 137–8
sightseeing 116–17
sizes (clothes) 52, 141
smoking requisites 48–9
snacks 23, 35, 83–4
sport 20, 23, 116, 117–18

stamps, postage 48, 100, 101, 150
station (bus) 20, 112, 150
station (railway) 20, 112, 113, 150
stationery 46, 47
sun protection 44, 46, 47
supermarket 23, 54, 66–8
sweets 64, 65, 68, 150
swimming pool 23, 35, 113, 116

taxi 23, 31, 112, 114
teeth 22, 92, 93, 94, 96
telegram 101
telephone 23, 40, 97, 102–3, 150
temperatures 140
tent 33, 34
theatre 23, 116
theft 98–9
tickets (travel) 14, 112, 114, 150
times 29, 30, 31, 32, 94–5, 96, 115, 116–17, 128–9
tobacconist 23, 48–9
toilet 23, 35, 38, 40, 82, 87, 117, 121, 123
toiletries 42–3
tourist information office 21, 26–7, 112, 123

town buildings 21
traffic police 97
train 25, 123
  destinations 112–13
  information 112
  times 26, 112
tram 25, 114
transport, public 25, 112–15
travel, *see* airport, bus, car etc.
travel agent 23, 104
travellers' cheques 59, 99
tyres (car) 107

underground 113, 122

valuables, loss or theft of 98–9
vegetables 67, 68, 70, 72–4
verbs 148–9
voltage 38

water 38, 39, 80, 122
weight guide 61, 63, 65, 69–70, 72, 73, 75, 77
weights 56, 139
wine 67, 81, 86, 87, 144, 145, 146, 147

youth hostel 23, 33–7

zoo 23, 116

Notes

Notes

Notes